Teaching
as a Human Activity

Ways to Make Classrooms
Joyful and Effective

Teaching
as a Human Activity

Ways to Make Classrooms
Joyful and Effective

By

J. Amos Hatch
University of Tennessee

Information Age Publishing, Inc.
Charlotte, North Carolina • www.infoagepub.com

Library of Congress Cataloging-in-Publication Data:

CIP data for this book can be found on the Library of Congress website:
http://www.loc.gov/index.html

Paperback: 978-1-64802-638-6
Hardcover: 978-1-64802-639-3
E-Book: 978-1-64802-640-9

Printed in the United States of America.

DEDICATION

For Breann Marie Hatch and Blair Alexandra Hatch

CONTENTS

PART III.
HOW CAN I MAKE MY CLASSROOM MANAGEMENT EFFECTIVE WHILE ENCOURAGING MY STUDENTS TO BECOME SELF-REGULATING AGENTS OF THEIR OWN BEHAVIOR?

PART IV.
WHAT ARE INSTRUCTIONAL APPROACHES THAT WILL ENGAGE MY STUDENTS IN SHAPING THEIR OWN DEVELOPMENT AND LEARNING?

PART V.
WHAT CAN I DO TO ENSURE MY SUCCESSFUL INITIATION
INTO THE TEACHING PROFESSION AND AVOID
BURNOUT IN THE FUTURE?

INTRODUCTION

Who Is Guarding the Meaning?

This is a book for teachers, especially new and soon-to-be teachers. It is a book from one teacher to other teachers who care deeply about what goes on in schools, who see teaching as a calling, who want to make their time in classrooms life changing for the students they are lucky enough to teach. This book is meant to inspire as much as instruct.

I just retired after over 45 years of teaching children, future teachers, and in-service teachers. I loved that work. It was my good fortune to share my love of teaching with hundreds of likeminded individuals along the way. As I taught in several public schools and at two universities, I learned lots of important lessons that are almost never addressed in textbooks for teachers. These are lessons that take teaching beyond the theory and practice addressed in teacher education coursework. These are lessons that accelerate school achievement at the same time they energize students to become engaged in what really matters: *learning itself*. These are lessons that tap into teachers' desire to have a meaningful connection to their students, lessons that give teachers the opportunity to experience the joy they imagined when they selected teaching as a career. Twenty of these lessons make up the substance of this book.

This book celebrates the passion, commitment, and intelligence that teachers bring to their profession. Bright, caring individuals are called to teaching because they feel a powerful drive to touch the lives of young people and to make a difference in the world (Nieto, 2014). The approaches advocated in these pages seek to take advantage of the commitment, drive, and brainpower teachers bring to their avocation. The

Teaching as a Human Activity: Ways to Make Classrooms Joyful and Effective
pp. xi–xiv

lessons explored foreground the humanity of teaching and highlight ways teachers can experience the satisfaction of sharing meaningful, learning-filled connections with their students.

I believe children and young people yearn for experiences that go beyond the mundane skill-based instruction and test-driven motivation that dominates classroom life in many schools. I know teachers want use their intelligence, energy, and creativity to enliven classroom learning. This book is about how to do that, while still meeting the expectations of the system. It is about doing your job, and at the same time, making that job more fulfilling, joyful, and meaningful for you and your students.

In the early 1980s, I took a sabbatical leave from my elementary school teaching duties to work on a doctoral degree. I had been teaching for 10 years in urban schools in Kansas City, Missouri and Jacksonville, Florida. I was not looking to leave the classroom. I did the advanced degree because I wanted to be a better teacher, I loved learning new stuff, and I wanted to be sure to use up the remaining G.I. Bill credit I had earned serving in the U.S. Army. Working full time on my PhD and being surrounded by really smart folks who cared about education as much as I did gave me the opportunity to spend time reflecting on and writing about what I thought I knew about teaching, learning, and schooling. I went back to elementary teaching for 2 years after the sabbatical, but my experiences in grad school led me to want to try to impact my profession as a scholar and teacher educator. Leaving the classroom was one of the hardest things I've ever done. I felt I had abandoned my calling for the first 3 or 4 years, but I moved into higher education and found a different kind of fulfillment teaching other teachers and adding to the knowledge base in my field.

One of my first publications in graduate school was entitled: "Who's Guarding the Meaning?" (Hatch, 1985). The thesis of the article was teachers were becoming estranged from providing meaningful instruction because of outside forces such as educational systems focused on technology (not the substance to be learned), loss of identity in the role of teacher (teaching is *what you do*, not *who you are*), and the denial of professional status (teachers are expected to be technicians, not decisionmakers). The article called on teachers, administrators and educational researchers to take responsibility for making meaningful instruction the defining quality of what goes on in schools.

Over 30 years later, the basic arguments in this essay hold up pretty well. I still think educators are the ones who must take responsibility for guarding the meaning in schools. My latest book, *Reclaiming the Teaching Profession: Transforming the Dialogue on Public Education* (Hatch, 2015) makes that same case in the context of today's educational milieu. What's missing in the 2015 book and what was missing in the 1985 article are specific strategies that future and new teachers can enact to accentuate the place of human interaction and meaning making in their classrooms. This book fills that space.

I see teaching as the most important role in society. I see teaching as an inherently human activity that provides a special opportunity for one person to have a profound impact on the life of another. I see teaching as a career that can fulfill educators' deepest desires to do work that is satisfying and makes a difference in the world around them.

I have been super lucky to work for over 30 years with hundreds of future and current teachers who came to education because their hearts and minds called them to touch the lives of children and young people. I worked in programs that attracted strong students who had to compete for slots in our teacher education programs. These were students who could have had successful in careers that offered much more money and prestige than teaching; but they selected education because they wanted their time at work to make a difference, to mean something beyond cashing a big check, to contribute something important to society, and to impact the lives of other human beings in positive ways.

Throughout my experiences as a classroom teacher and teacher educator, I have collected strategies and ways of being in classrooms that have proven to make teachers' and students' experiences more human, more engaging, and more successful. This little book is a detailed description of 20 of these humanizing approaches. I do not see these as "tricks of the trade." For me and teachers I have worked with, these ways of operating in classrooms are touchstones that keep educators heading in a direction that energizes the school lives of students and fulfills teachers' desires to do important work that makes a difference. The lessons in this book are the opposite of gimmicks; they are alternative ways of thinking about and being in the classroom. They build on teachers' intelligence, commitment, and desire to touch the lives of others.

Over the years, I have shared (some would say *preached*) these "lessons" (and others like them) alongside the traditional curriculum of knowledge and skills that all teacher education students get. The 20 explored here are the ones that most ring true for teachers once they get into the field. My hope is that by considering each of these classroom mindsets one at a time, future and current educators will see clear connections between why they came to teaching in the first place and what they can accomplish in real classrooms.

In each chapter, I lay out a rationale for why the approach being described is important to teaching that can ignite a shared joy of learning. I give examples of how the ideas presented have been implemented and detail procedures for walking the walk in real classrooms. I do not ignore the pressing realities that define contemporary teaching; I offer ways to accomplish the goals of the system while building classroom cultures that facilitate genuine, meaningful, joyful engagement with learning. I write as if we are colleagues talking face to face about what's important in our work and how to be more effective at bringing the centrality of human connections back to the classroom.

The lessons that make up the body of this book are organized around five questions that every teacher needs to consider:

1. What can I do to be sure I realize my dream of making a positive difference in the lives of my students?
2. How can I make my teaching effective by building on vital human connections with my students?
3. How can I make my classroom management effective, while encouraging my students to become self-regulating agents of their own behavior?
4. What are instructional approaches that will engage my students in shaping their own development and learning?
5. What can I do to ensure my successful initiation into the teaching profession and avoid burnout in the future?

Four lessons are included in each of the five parts defined by these questions.

This book asks seriously: Who is guarding the meaning in the first quarter of the 21st century? My premise is it is up to teachers to bring meaning to their individual classrooms. Guarding the meaning is an opportunity and an obligation. We have the opportunity to make learning an exciting and invaluable human experience. We have the obligation to our students and our society to connect to the soul of teaching, to do our best to create an expansive vision of learning for ourselves and our students. We have the opportunity and the obligation to redefine teaching as an inherently joyful human activity. I hope you will join me in taking on this challenge and that the ideas in this book will inspire your commitment and support your efforts to become the best teacher you can be.

REFERENCES

Hatch, J. A. (1985). Who's guarding the meaning? Thoughts on the erosion of professional commitment. *Journal of Humanistic Education, 9,* 4–8.

Hatch, J. A. (2015). *Reclaiming the teaching profession: Transforming the dialogue on public education.* Rowman & Littlefield.

Nieto, S. (Ed.). (2014). *Why teach now.* Teachers College Press.

PART I

WHAT CAN I DO TO BE SURE I REALIZE MY DREAM OF MAKING A POSITIVE DIFFERENCE IN THE LIVES OF MY STUDENTS?

CHAPTER 1

OUR GOAL SHOULD BE TO MAKE A DIFFERENCE IN THE LIFE OF EVERY STUDENT WE TEACH

I was a teacher educator at the University of Tennessee for 30 years. We did not allow just anyone who showed up to enter our program. We believed that teacher preparation should look like the training provided in other professional fields. We offered teacher licensure coursework at the masters degree level once students had earned bachelors degrees in an arts and sciences major. We placed students in cohorts and worked with them for a year and a half, including a full-year's internship in public schools. We had rigorous standards for being considered for our teacher education programs, and no one was admitted without answering a set of complex questions on a written application and sitting before an interview board that included teacher education faculty, local school personnel, and advanced graduate students. We had a limited number of slots available, and during some years, more than half of all applicants were turned away.

I estimate I must have read the applications of and interviewed well over 600 students who were seeking admission during my time at Tennessee. By and large, the prospective teachers who made it to the application and interview stage were accomplished, smart folks who had lots of choices about what they could do with their careers. Most had a good idea of what teaching is all about, a strong commitment to touching the lives of

Teaching as a Human Activity: Ways to Make Classrooms Joyful and Effective
pp. 3–10
Copyright © 2021 by Information Age Publishing

young people, and a deep desire to have a positive impact on society (Phillips & Hatch, 2000). Most wrote articulate responses to the open-ended questions on the application, and most were able to express themselves well during their high-stakes interviews.

I believed in the importance of this screening process and worked hard to be fair to the applicants, while being cognizant of the impact of my decisions on the future of the profession. Over the years, I observed some patterns in students' responses. Most of the repeated phrases were positive and made perfect sense (e.g., "I love children" and "I've known I wanted to teach since I was a child"). Some sent up potential red flags (e.g., "I want to teach until my spouse earns enough money so we can start a family" or "I like that you get weekends and summers off"). One response that was used by both successful and unsuccessful candidates became a kind of pet peeve for me. I am not sure where they got it, but many said or wrote something like: "I know I will not make a lot of money teaching, but if I can make a difference in the life of just one student, it will all be worth it."

It sounds good on its face, and I get the first part. These candidates knew that they could make more money by taking the same 5 years we required and going to grad school in business or a professional field other than teaching. But, imagining that touching the life of one young person will fulfill your career seems like a pretty minimal aspiration. I know it is only a catchphrase—a good-sounding generalization—but expecting to make a difference in the life of just one student is aiming way too low. That is what makes teaching such an exciting and energizing occupational choice: we have the opportunity to change the life of each and every young person with whom we work. Making all our students' lives better is not a byproduct of what we to; it is the heart and soul of our job!

It is widely acknowledged that teaching is among the most stressful occupations (Wiggins, 2015). One reason it is stressful is that you have to make hundreds of decisions on the fly every day—decisions that matter. Other professionals see one client or patient at a time and have as much time as they need to process information, consult with others, and make decisions. Teachers face 20 or 30 (sometimes more) students at once and make decisions and take action on the spot that impact everyone involved in or observing that action. Teachers need special knowledge and skills to make good decisions. Quality teacher preparation can give new teachers the tools and confidence they need to survive, even when classrooms become stressful. But, what about *thriving* in school settings? What about addressing why we became teachers in the first place? What about enriching the lived experience of the children we teach? What about making a genuine difference in the life of every student we can? Yes, teaching can be stressful; but when we touch other human lives in positive ways, teaching can be joyful and fulfilling like no other kind of work can ever be.

As my own career unfolded, having a positive impact on those I had the privilege to teach changed from an unspoken aim to the foundational goal on which my professional practice was built. In my 13-plus years in elementary classrooms, I tried to constantly remind myself that the reason I was there was to improve the life chances of the children with whom I shared six or seven hours each day. In my university teaching, I made myself focus and refocus on what I could do to help my students become better learners, more complete people, and stronger teachers.

In both public school and university settings, it was easy to let the day-to-day grind of what the system expected of me and my students get in the way of what really matters: supporting the development of confident, competent, caring people. It is hard to see the trees when the forest that surrounds teaching is so dense. But paying deliberate attention to the capacities, needs, and strengths of individual students from preschool through graduate studies is imperative if you plan to make a positive difference in their lives.

The closer I got to the end of my active career as an educator, the more deliberate my attention to individual development became. Many times, events occurred that called for immediate action on my part. For example, one especially promising teacher intern felt devastated when she received lower than expected marks on the nationally normed performance assessment needed for teacher licensure in our state. She began to doubt her ability to teach and started to question her decision to enter the profession. Our program had a procedure in place to make it possible for her to earn her license; but she needed more than a piece of paper that said she could be hired. So it became important for me to provide experiences, feedback, and unconditional support to let her know she was a promising new teacher who would have a wonderfully successful career. This meant having a long face-to-face talk around the theme: "You are the same person and the same great teacher you were the day before those test results came back." It meant making sure she recognized all the positive feedback she had accumulated from her professors, peers, students, parents and mentor teachers that went beyond a set of numbers from an assessment, in my words, "scored by some invisible someone grinding through piles of papers in another state."

When there is a crisis like the one described, it is evident that teaching needs to be more than preparing folks for the next assessment. But, the enormity of the many tasks that teachers have to complete makes it hard to be aware of the needs of all the students in their charge. During the last years of my university career, I would make myself study a roster of my teacher education students, assess my interactions with each of them, and actively plan for ways to positively impact their lives.

One example that comes to mind involves a nontraditional teacher education student who emitted vibes that since she was older and had kids of her own, she was way ahead of the younger students in her cohort and did not have much to learn from her peers (or her professors or mentor teachers in the schools). So, I needed a plan that accentuated the maturity and experience she brought to the program, while helping her see how much she could benefit from learning from others. The goal was not to blame her for thinking she did not have anything to learn; I wanted to help her see how she was being perceived by those around her. I started with the assumption that she wanted to become the strongest teacher she could be, and then used specific events to show her how others might misinterpret her verbal and nonverbal actions. Just monitoring how she was coming across to others helped her change her behavior and her relationships with those around her.

Another very bright student who grew up in a rural East Tennessee setting used patterns of speech that were fine at home but would not provide a good example for her future students or be appropriate for written or spoken communication with parents or other professionals (especially in job interview settings). This plan involved helping her become aware of her speech patterns as differences (not deficiencies), see the need for being able to code switch in professional settings, practice so she could adjust her speech when needed, and use videotapes of her teaching to monitor her improvement (which was dramatic).

I have been lucky enough to observe many of my preservice teachers make human connections with students that go beyond the standard curriculum. One intern saw an opportunity to use her skills as an elite soccer player and fluent Spanish speaker to become the volunteer coach of a start-up team that included many of the recently emigrated Guatemalan boys in her class. Another preservice teacher spent out-of-school time making music with the grandmother who was raising a boy in her class and who was an accomplished bluegrass musician. Experiences like those of Sadie and Beth generate relationships that make teaching an exciting human activity. They benefit everyone involved.

When I was teaching elementary school, I made a particular effort to not forget the quiet kids in my classes—the ones who did everything that was expected and did not stand out (for positive or negative reasons). For example, I remember coaching and demonstrating how to enter a play group with other children when I observed a kindergarten child who appeared to want to join with others but did not know how or did not possess the willingness to risk rejection. The coaching part was to just explain what I do when I want to enter a group that has already formed; the demonstrating was to actually ask a group of children if I could play with them.

In all these teaching settings, I was adding academic value by doing my best to teach the curriculum; but the point here is that I was intentionally adding value to students' lives in a much bigger sense. For me, trying to make a meaningful difference is what I was there for; and that is what makes teaching the most important occupation I can imagine. In both school and college settings, I sometimes failed. No matter my good intentions, I sometimes misread the situation, had an inadequate plan, or set myself an impossible goal. Some of these failures haunt me to this day. I remember working for months to do everything I could to show a second grade boy that he could rely on me to provide stability and predictability that he lacked in the rest of his life, only to throw it all away in a moment of anger when I yelled, "What are you thinking?" after he took the report card of another student and ditched his own behind a filing cabinet. I vividly remember the crestfallen look in his eyes that said, "You're just like all the rest."

You will not be successful every time you try to help someone move forward with his or her life; we all make mistakes, and some asks are just too big. But if you have done your level best, you will be able to look yourself in the eye and know that you have made a difference for your students and the society we need to protect and improve. What more could you ask of yourself or your chosen profession?

Another frequent response when prospective teachers were applying for admission into our program went something like: "I want my students to remember me like I remember my _____ teacher, Mr. or Ms. _____." When asked to say why they remember a particular teacher, virtually every applicant talked about a human connection that went way beyond the grade level or subject matter being taught (e.g., "She knew my family was going through a divorce and gave me extra attention at school" or "He stayed after school to meet with me to make sure I was able to keep up in calculus").

Being remembered for good reasons helps make my point about the vital importance of human contact in making a difference in students' lives. Still, I worry that teachers are vulnerable and a little naïve when we depend on being remembered as a measure of our impact. I tried to help the future teachers with whom I worked see that being remembered should not be the ultimate goal.

I love to hear from former students. I am even online friends with a few of my elementary students from years ago. But, as I have told my university students, even if their students do not remember them or anything specific about what happened in their classrooms, that does not mean that what happened there did not impact their lives in meaningful ways. I do not think there is any such thing as "water under the bridge" in teaching. I am saying that as teachers we have the awesome opportunity to touch lives in big and small ways—and we will have an impact, whether what we do or say is actively remembered or not.

My wife is a retired physical education teacher. She taught physical education to college, middle, and elementary school students. She was a dedicated professional and exceptionally accomplished at what she did. She was recognized as an outstanding teacher everywhere she worked. Deb and I have talked a lot about being remembered by our students. In her last job, she worked in a supersized elementary school where she taught hundreds of students each week. She sometimes lamented that her students would never remember her because she was spread so thin. My counter with her (and my university students) is that teachers will likely never know their true impact on their students; but that does not mean that the impact did not happen.

I remind Deb of all the times she went beyond the call of duty to be sure that every child benefited from her activities—no matter if they were developing their skills as high performers (some of whom have become college and professional athletes) or were kids with less natural ability (including children with disabilities). I try to help her recall all the times when what she was providing as a caring, competent professional was the most important experience in some child's day—times when a student felt a sense of pride, accomplishment and acceptance that was a scarce commodity in the rest of his or her life. Those feelings do not have to be stored in long-term memory to have made a difference.

As will be discussed in more depth in later chapters (especially Chapter 7), I am not talking here about being a "nice" teacher, "loving all my children," or being "everyone's favorite teacher." In and of themselves, being nice, loving children, and currying favor do not help young people's lives improve. In fact, these kinds of aspirations can get in the way when teachers make bad decisions in order to maintain their favored status with their students (Hatch, 1999). I am talking about being a competent, caring professional who knows how to use her or his humanity to connect with students in ways that enhance the innate capacities of those young people.

The worst case happens when teachers "love" their students so much that they feel sorry for their circumstances and stop expecting them to excel (Gershenson et al., 2016). Lots of kids you will teach face life situations that are difficult to imagine and impossible to ignore; but that's not a reason to expect less of them. It is a reason to dig in and find ways to give them opportunities to succeed and know they can be successful. That is what they want and that is what their parents want from you (Cepeda, 2016). Many times, I have heard myself tell new teachers in the voice of their students: "Don't love me so much. Teach me something!"

One of the themes of this book is that learning is an inherently valuable part of our humanity. I believe that teaching young people that learning is exciting, enriching, and fulfilling is our most important instructional task. This goes way beyond the curriculum that we have to teach to prepare kids for standardized tests. It is a way to truly touch the lives of our students. Yes, we need to be there for them in all the parts of their humanness—to support their growth in all the areas of development in all the ways we can. But, the most important gift we can give is for them to leave us knowing that learning is a vital part of being a fully functioning person and that each one of them is capable of experiencing the joy and satisfaction of being an able learner. Chapter 6 is all about how to do that.

I have sometimes felt discouraged because too much of what's happening in the current climate makes it hard to be positive (Hatch, 2015). But when I have spent time with real teachers in public school classrooms and looked into the eyes of the future teachers with whom I have been so blessed to work, I see a massive opportunity. I am hoping that this little book can help teachers take advantage of the chance to fulfill the desires and satisfy the needs that brought them to teaching in the first place.

I know teachers are in the profession to shape the future by touching the lives of others. I know that they long to have meaningful positive connections with those they teach. I know that they want to have a positive impact on the lives of as many young people as they possibly can. I want them to know that that's a realistic, achievable goal—not an easy goal, but one that can make a teaching career more fulfilling than any occupational choice imaginable. The rest of this book is designed to help educators live their dream of being a teacher who makes a powerful positive difference.

REFERENCES

Cepeda, E. J. (2016, April 19). Minority parents want schools to push their kids. *Albuquerque Journal.* https://www.abqjournal.com/.../minority-parents-want-schools-to-push-their-kids.html

Gershenson, S., Holt, S. B., & Papageorge, P. W. (2016). Who believes in me? The effect of student–teacher demographic match on teacher expectations. *Economics of Education Review, 52,* 209–224.

Hatch, J. A. (1999). What preservice teachers can learn from studies of teachers' work. *Teaching and Teacher Education, 15,* 229–242.

Hatch, J. A. (2015). *Reclaiming the teaching profession: Transforming the dialogue on public education.* Rowman & Littlefield.

Phillips, M. B., & Hatch, J. A. (2000). Why teach? Prospective teachers' reasons for entering the profession. *Journal of Early Childhood Teacher Education, 21,* 373–384.

Wiggins, K. (2015, June 25). *Teaching is among the top three most stressed occupations.* TES. https://www.tes.com/news/teaching-among-top-three-most-stressed-occupations

CHAPTER 2

STUDENTS NEED A PURPOSE TO GIVE ENERGY TO SCHOOLING

Whose school is it? Why do we have schools?

These are questions that ought to be at the center of every conversation about education in America, in our hometowns, and in our individual schools. Over the years, I have perpetually asked these questions of myself, my readers, and my students (from kindergartners to doctoral candidates). Getting a rousing conversation going around these questions is pretty easy. It is interesting to see the different takes that come up in these discussions; but what is most telling to me is the recognition that almost none of the folks who engage seriously with these questions have ever done so in the past. And what is most disconcerting to me is that almost none of the students and educators who participate in thinking seriously about these fundamental questions see the possibility of any change based on the answers they generate. It is like, "Sure these are critical questions that no one ever seems to raise; and yes things would surely look different in schools if we took some of our answers to heart; but so what?—the system is too entrenched and things are not going to change no matter what we say here today."

Whose school is it? Who does the school belong to? Who gets to decide what goes on in schools? The answers I have gotten to these questions range from, "The state has been given constitutional responsibility for the schooling of its citizens," to "Schools exist for children and young people,

Teaching as a Human Activity: Ways to Make Classrooms Joyful and Effective
pp. 11–18
Copyright © 2021 by Information Age Publishing

so it is their school." Between are arguments like, "Schools ought to reflect the values of local communities," "Teachers know best what is good for their students so they should be charge of schools," and "Parents pay the taxes that support the school, so they should have more say in how schools work." Then, there are those with more cynical perspectives who point to the status quo and argue that, "In reality, schools are *owned* by powerful politicians, wealthy philanthropists, and well-connected testing and publishing companies."

Why do we have schools? What is the purpose of schooling? What should schools be trying to accomplish? These questions also generate a variety of responses. I have heard answers from, "Schools exist to pass along American culture to the next generation" to "Schools are places for individuals to explore their interests and fulfill their own potential." Other answers include statements like, "Schools are responsible for training the workforce of the future," "We have schools to prepare knowledgeable citizens to participate in our democracy," and "The job of schools is to create good decision makers for a complex future." Critical students and educators sometimes make the case that, "Schooling is nothing more than a sorting mechanism that is in place to replicate the status quo, keeping rich folks rich and poor people in their place."

It is fascinating to think about how different life in and around schools could be depending on how folks answer the questions related to ownership, decision making, and purposes. And that is the point of asking what is almost never asked. It is easy to treat discussions like this as pedantic activities that take us nowhere; but I am hoping to get you thinking about ways you as a future or practicing teacher can act with integrity and confidence to make a difference based on how you answer these foundational questions. Ultimately, I want to suggest strategies for engaging your students in taking more ownership of their education and for helping them see meaningful purposes for being in school every day.

I have taught in several schools and visited many more over the years, most of these being urban public schools in underserved communities. As a teacher, researcher, and preservice teacher supervisor, I have been in hundreds of classrooms for thousands of hours. One of the things that has stunned me over the years is the persistent realization that the students (preschool through high school) had no sense of purpose for being there. The did not know why they were there other than that is what everyone did and that is what the adults in their lives said they had to do. More often than I like to think about, their teachers' notions of why they were there seemed almost as obtuse. In fact, many seemed more focused on maintaining order and keeping kids busy than on trying to accomplish some educational or social purpose. I say this not to blame these teachers, but to point out how far afield we get when we are not able to articulate a worthy purpose for what we do.

Another way to examine the purposes of school is to imagine metaphors that provide an alternative lens for thinking about how schools work. Again, I like to get future teachers and graduate students (most of whom have been practicing educators) to use their metaphoric thinking capacities (see Chapter 14) to generate different visions of education. Many interesting comparisons have come up over the years. Some positive, for example: schools as gardens; schools as community centers; schools as families; and schools as democracies. Some that cast schooling in a more negative light include: schools as factories; schools as babysitters; schools as acculturation agencies; and schools as total institutions (like prisons and asylums).

So, just to get you thinking, imagine the differences in the role of teachers and students when you conceptualize schools as gardens as opposed to schools as factories. What would teachers spend their time doing in order to nurture their students' growth in a garden school compared to what they would do on a factory assembly line? How would students think about why they were there and what they were supposed to do in these different metaphoric circumstances? How would you decide whether or not you had been successful in each of these settings?

For me, it is intellectually fun to think in these unusual ways about what educators face every day; but I am more interested in what kind of impressions we come away with regarding the purposes of real schools. We can play with ideas and come up with interesting reasons to think schools should be more like democracies than prisons; but what does that mean for our careers as front line workers in the real world of education?

I think it means that teachers need to know what we think the purposes of schooling ought to be and that we need to help our students come to a shared understanding of what schools are for and why they are there. As my writing about teaching has evolved (e.g., Hatch, 2005, 2015; Hatch & Conrath, 1988), I have offered an array of aims that I count as legitimate purposes of schooling. I have always said that there are many worthy purposes and that we do not have to settle on only one. But, if we do not know why we are there and our students see no compelling purpose for being there, the school experience will be vapid at best and chaotic at worst.

What are some worthy purposes? Do students and teachers need to share the same aims? You have to decide for yourself what makes a purpose worthy or not (and I will give you some options that I think are salient in today's schools); but, to answer the second question first: Yes, I believe you and your students need to be on the same page and have a shared vision of why you are doing what you do for all those hours every day. There is a reason that the term "cross purposes" is part of everyday lexicon. People cannot work in harmony when they find themselves at cross purposes. Things do not get done when people find themselves at cross purposes. Conflicts are inevitable when people find themselves at cross purposes. More later on how to facilitate the creation of shared purposes in real classrooms. For now, here is an overview of three worthy purposes to consider.

COOPERATION AS THE PURPOSE OF SCHOOLING

Rodman Webb changed my life while I was a doctoral student at the University of Florida. He flipped my view of what research was and could be and opened my eyes to the profound relationship between schooling and society. Rod was a professor who taught his readers and his students to think deeply about educational aims and how important they are to conceptualizing and doing school (Webb, 1981). He planted an intellectual seed in me that grew into an important part of my own teaching and writing. One of the aims that he got me thinking about was cooperation.

Rod argued that the ability and willingness to cooperate were undervalued in society and schools (Webb, 1981). He pointed out that cooperation is mostly taken for granted, but that it is essential for the perpetuation of a sustainable and just society. He contrasted the potential benefits of emphasizing cooperation as an educational aim with society's obsession with competition and individuality, which is reflected in how schools are organized and what we ask students to endure. Professor Webb was all about unpacking assumptions and looking beneath the surface of what goes on in school. I agree with him that when you examine what students learn about the value of competition versus cooperation, the hidden curriculum of schooling sends the tacit, pervasive message that cooperation is an afterthought at best and competition is the coin of the realm. Educators could turn that around (or at least bring about more balance) by adopting a thoughtful approach to teaching and learning that emphasized cooperation as an explicit purpose of education. This is not an impossible ask for teachers. Just applying some of the expansive and compelling literature on cooperative learning (e.g., Gillies, 2007; Johnson, 2009; Schul, 2012) would be a promising place to start.

MAXIMIZING INDIVIDUAL CAPABILITIES AS THE PURPOSE OF SCHOOLING

When I did my undergraduate teacher preparation at the University of Utah, it was an explicit aim of the program that our teaching should facilitate the fulfillment of human potential in our students. Of course, that was before the powerful forces behind the education reform movement changed the face of education to a laser focus on market-based accountability via standards and test scores (Hatch, 2015). Still today, when future teachers talk about why they want to enter the profession, they never say, "To prepare students to score well on standardized tests" or "To train students to be productive workers." They want to teach so they can, "Help children become all they can be" or "Give students a chance to fulfill their dreams."

Teachers' aspirations for their teaching careers actually align with what is almost always written in the statements of purpose or mission statements that all schools have. These documents always say something like, "We are committed to teaching the whole child and providing all children with optimal educational opportunities so they can maximize their potential." They never say, "We believe in stressing academics so the most able will rise above the rest." No matter the realities of contemporary schooling, how individual teachers and schools think about what they can do to enhance the life chances of students should be paramount. If we are convinced that our primary mission is to support each student's search for self-fulfillment, then we must engage in behavior that matches our commitment.

Again, we are not left to our wits to figure out how to make schools and classrooms match up more closely with our personal and professional commitments to supporting students' healthy development. There is a powerful history and well-established literature on teaching the whole child (e.g., Miller, 2010; Noddings, 2005), whose basic principles are as salient today as ever. Further, there is contemporary guidance for designing programs and school experiences that enhance children's chances of fulfilling their potential. To expand one promising example, the *capability approach* (Adair, 2014; Buzzelli, 2020) provides a model for teaching and learning based on the assumption that children's abilities are "capacities rather than commodities" (Buzzelli, 2020, p. 168). The capability approach shifts the focus from assessing schools and teachers based how well they produce measurable outcomes to how well we expand students' well being and free agency. As can be seen in this example, even though it has been around for a long time and has taken on new language, maximizing human potential is still a worthy goal of education.

EDUCATING FOR A DEMOCRACY OF THE INTELLECT AS THE PURPOSE OF SCHOOLING

When I was a new assistant professor at the Ohio State University campus in Marion, I became friends and tennis partners with Jack Conrath, who was then an assistant superintendent in the Marion City Schools system.

Jack and I had the opportunity to hear a speech delivered by Ralph Tyler, whom many count as the father of modern curriculum theory. Tyler talked about the important contributions education had made to our democratic way of life since Jefferson's time. Jack and I talked about the speech off and on for several weeks and decided to write an article that summarized our thinking about what schools could and should be in order to keep alive the democratic legacy Tyler described. In the piece, we called for making "educating for a democracy of the intellect" (Hatch & Conrath, 1988, p. 44) a central purpose of schooling in the United States.

Dr. Conrath and I adapted the term "democracy of the intellect" from Jacob Bronowski's (1973) classic description of the evolution of Western culture, *The Ascent of Man*. Bronowski argued that the survival of our democratic way of life is dependent on each person's responsible participation in the decisions that shape our future. Such decision making, he said, requires every person (not just so called experts) to take responsibility for knowing what our world is like and how it works. In our article, Jack and I argued that schools had the chance to improve students' democratic intellect and to help them see the importance of applying "informed integrity" (Hatch & Conrath, 1988, p. 44) to their actions.

Forty years on, educating for a democracy of the intellect still seems like a worthwhile purpose of our profession. In fact, given the current political climate at this writing, it seems like giving future citizens the tools they need to be willing and able participants in democratic decision making is more important than ever. As an essential component of that effort, students need to be shown that they can be critical consumers of information—to be able to discern fact from fiction, truth from propaganda, unbiased reporting from "fake news." Further, young people need to feel empowered to put their democratic intelligence into action. If we care about the future of our way of life, one way to help improve our chances would be to adopt as an aim of schooling the development of a democracy of the intellect in our students.

These three examples are just that: examples. Many other purposes are worthy of being guiding forces for what we do in school. In fact, many of the chapters in the first four sections of this book could form the basis for a salient aim of education (see especially Chapters 6, 8, and 14). The big idea here is that we need to have a shared sense of purpose in order for school to make sense for us and the young people we teach.

Too many classrooms I have observed seem to be set up as battlegrounds because students (and some teachers) have no idea why they are actually there. Inert ideas are piled on inert ideas, without meaningful connection to anything real. Students figure out the school game very early in their education careers. Some opt to play along; some do just enough to get by; and some actively resist what they see as a waste of their time. Students and teachers need a genuine, meaningful purpose for doing what they do in school. They need a shared sense that their time in schools has meaning beyond compulsory attendance, preparing for the test, or moving on to the next grade level. So, what can teachers do to develop a shared sense of purpose in their classrooms?

The first element that has to be in place is for you to identify a core purpose that you can believe in. If you do not buy in, your students will see right through your charade. When I told my kindergartners that we were the "K Learning Team" and we were going to "learn a little every day," that is exactly what I meant. When I told my teacher candidates that our program would prepare them to be effective teachers in schools with the highest needs and fewest resources, I did not blink. In fact, I always added that we were preparing them to be successful and *to stay* in urban-multicultural schools.

Believing in your own narrative is necessary but not sufficient. You need to *tell* your students what you see as the raison d'être for schooling, and you need to *show* them what that purpose means for how you do school every day. Telling your students what you think is your school's reason for being means saying it early and often. It means introducing your purpose at the earliest opportunity and reminding your students again and again. Telling also means putting it in writing on bulletin boards, syllabi, letters to parents, and any other print or graphic forms available.

Even more important than telling is making sure your students see how your purpose drives what happens in our classroom. Unless you show students how your educational aim is enacted, it will turn into an empty slogan. That is part of the power of bulletin boards and classroom graphics (e.g., you can point to the board that says, "Learn a Little Every Day" and celebrate with the students every time the light goes off in someone's head and genuine learning has occurred). That is why you make explicit links between the purposes named on your classroom web page and the activities you post there (e.g., you can show students why completing a community mapping project provides invaluable insights into becoming a successful urban-multicultural teacher).

We live in a complex world, and schools are complex settings. That complexity means that education fulfills many purposes, some competing and some complementary. The main idea of this chapter is that students need to see some meaningful purpose for giving energy to their school experience. Without a sense of shared purpose, it is hard to imagine how students and teachers can accomplish as much as they can when everyone knows why they are there and what outcomes are desirable. School does not have to be a tug of war between teachers and students. If everyone is pulling together in an effort to reach a shared objective, everyone can share in the inherent joy of doing meaningful work and doing it well.

REFERENCES

Adair, J. K. (2014). Agency and expanding capacities in the early grades: What it could mean for young children in the early grades. *Harvard Educational Review, 84*(2), 217–241).

Bronowski, J. (1973). *The ascent of man*. Little Brown and Company.

Buzzelli, C. A. (2020). Changing the discourse: The capability approach and early childhood education. In J. J. Mueller & N. File (Eds.), *Curriculum in early childhood education: Re-examined, reclaimed, renewed* (pp. 161–176). Routledge.

Gillies, R. (2007). *Cooperative learning: Integrating theory and practice*. SAGE.

Hatch, J. A. (2005). *Teaching in the new kindergarten*. Delmar.

Hatch, J. A. (2015). *Reclaiming the teaching profession: Transforming the dialogue on public education*. Rowman & Littlefield.

Hatch, J. A., & Conrath, J. M. (1988). Refocusing the identity of schooling: Education for a democracy of the intellect. *Kappa Delta Pi Record, 24*(1), 41–45.

Johnson, D. W. (2009). An educational psychology success story: Social interdependence theory and cooperative learning. *Educational Researcher, 38*(5), 365–379.

Miller, J. P. (2010). *Whole child education*. University of Toronto Press.

Noddings, N. (2005). What does it mean to educate the whole child? *Educational Leadership, 63*(1), 8–13.

Schul, J. E. (2012). Revisiting an old friend: The practice and promise of cooperative learning for the twenty-first century. *The Social Studies, 102*, 88–93.

Webb, R. B. (1981). *Schooling and society*. Macmillan.

CHAPTER 3

CLASSROOMS NEED TO BE PLACES WHERE EVERYONE HAS A STAKE IN EVERYONE ELSE'S SUCCESS

It is a familiar trope that classrooms should be learning communities, but it is hard to find places where such communities are the order of the day. In fact, building a sense that everyone in the classroom has responsibility for the success of everyone else turns out to be an invaluable approach to setting up and managing classrooms. When students see real meaning in their daily activity and they learn that there is genuine satisfaction in sharing the quest for success with their peers, interactions in the classroom take on a powerful positive tenor. Even within systems set up to reward and punish students based on narrow definitions of performance, classroom communities can be established that send the overriding message that meaningful learning is what is valued here, there is more than enough success so that everyone can have a share, and we all excel when each of us excels. This chapter describes real classroom communities, gives examples of why they work, and details steps to making them happen.

This chapter builds on the last because having a shared sense of purpose is central to building a team culture in which all the players—teachers and students—have a stake in everyone else's success. When students and teachers are at cross purposes, there is no reason to pull together as a

Teaching as a Human Activity: Ways to Make Classrooms Joyful and Effective
pp. 19–26
Copyright © 2021 by Information Age Publishing
All rights of reproduction in any form reserved.

team. When students see themselves as individuals in competition with other students, there is reason to be threatened by the success of others. So, there needs to be a reason for being in school that goes beyond sorting children and young people in stratified groups based on performance. Establishing classroom purposes like those mentioned in Chapter 2 provides a necessary platform on which to build a viable classroom community.

Maybe because being in sports was a life saver for me when I was a kid, I have tried to create a team mentality in all of the classrooms in which I have taught. Sometimes, we explicitly called ourselves a team, as in "We are the K Team" or "We are the 4th Grade Learning Team." Sometimes, we set ourselves apart by delineating how different we were from other classes around us, as in "We will work together to become the best class in this elementary school" or "As a teacher education cohort, we have special commitments and specialized instruction, so we will become special teachers." As in sports, the emphasis in our thinking about each other and what we were all about always emphasized the word "We."

I know some of you may be put off by the sports metaphor or the notion of being in competition with other classes; but I hope you will not dismiss the importance of building a shared sense of community. Even if you prefer different metaphors (e.g., orchestras, teams of scientists, dance ensembles) or do not connect to a specific metaphor at all, the opportunity to bring your students together as a cooperative unit should not be overlooked. And you do not have to create imaginary competitive antagonists to engender the overriding sense that "We are in this together" or "We can accomplish great things if we have each others' backs." No matter how you approach it, creating a genuine classroom community will mean you are taking a giant leap toward making your classroom a place that feels better, operates more efficiently, and accomplishes more.

It feels better to be part of a classroom where everyone senses that he or she is an integral part of a team that has an important mission to accomplish. It is not hard to spot the kids in any classroom who are alienated from their peers, teachers, and the expectations of school. My experience is that these disaffected students come in two basic types. The first set is composed of those who do their best to disengage from anything to do with school. They slump in their seats, make eye contact with no one, never raise their hands or speak up in class, and do as little as possible to complete their assigned school tasks. The second group takes the opposite approach. Instead of trying to disappear in class, these students intentionally call attention to themselves by challenging the teacher, annoying their peers, openly refusing to do their school work, and generally being disruptive.

Both kinds of reactions are troublesome and generate a lot of stress in classrooms. There are multiple potential social and psychological explanations for both passive withdrawal and aggressive resistance, and it is extra complex for teachers because they have to deal with the issues that arise from these behaviors while teaching the rest of the students. I am not promising that building a classroom community will make issues like these disappear; but I am sure that when an ethos of caring and shared responsibility is created, classrooms will be places where fewer students will be alienated from each other, their teachers, and the curriculum.

Try to put yourself in the heads of students you know. When they get up in the morning and think about their day, do they think of school as a place where they are valued and supported, a place where they have important work to do, and a place where they get to share in the successes of other children they care about? Or, do they think of their classroom as a place where they feel the threat of being humiliated, a place where they waste a lot of time on meaningless busywork, or a place where someone else's success means that their chances of succeeding have been reduced? School feels energizing to children and young people in the former group; it feels enervating to those in the later. How do students you know feel?

How students feel and think about school shapes their behavior in profound ways. We should be doing all we can to set up classrooms that students look forward to sharing with other people they care about. Nel Noddings (1995, 2013) has written extensively about the critical importance of applying an ethic of care in schools. She has long argued that caring communities of learning are essential to young people's overall wellbeing and their academic success. In her words:

> My contention is, first, that we should want more from our educational efforts than adequate academic achievement and, second, that we will not achieve even that meager success unless our children believe that they themselves are cared for and learn to care for others. (Noddings, 1995, p. 675)

They do not just feel better, classrooms operate better when children know why they are there, when they care about themselves and others, and when they share a commitment to supporting the success of those around them. If you have spent any time in real classrooms, you know that a smoothly running day is essential to student success, teacher effectiveness, and an overall lack of stress. Without having a learning community in place, classrooms take on the risk of being reduced to sites of ongoing struggle, where teachers spend more time resolving conflicts than teaching. Building a classroom community does not guarantee that your days will run perfectly, but establishing a shared commitment to working together to accomplish a common goal creates the superstructure on which efficient operating procedures can be attached.

So, what are some of the elements that make a classroom a community of learners—elements that make teachers' days operate smoothly? As I have argued for the last two chapters, having a shared sense of purpose is the first and most important element. Building on that keystone means establishing routines, rules and rituals that provide students with the security of knowing what is expected and what to do when things get off track. It also means helping students develop the social skills they need to optimize their participation in a caring community of learners (Levine, 2003).

Establishing procedures and routines are essential in any setting in which people have to work together to accomplish a shared task. If individuals have to spend time every day negotiating what they will do, when, and with whom, more time will be spent figuring all that out than on the task itself. Good teachers have always set up predictable schedules to signal what will happen when, and for how long. They also establish routines for accomplishing the mundane but necessary elements of school life (e.g., transitions from one activity to the next, distributing materials, preparing for end of class/end of day, restroom breaks, etc.). It is hard to imagine any classroom running efficiently without well-established procedures and routines, and that is certainly true for classroom communities.

I give a full chapter (Chapter 10) to discussing the important place of rules, so I will not go deeply here. Suffice it to say that in a community of learners who share a common view of their reason for being there, rules will build directly on their shared connections and the central importance of supporting each other in the realization of their shared purpose. So goals will be shaped not by the treat of punishment but by the compelling need to not detract from the aims of the group. And consequences will not depend on applying the power of the teacher but on aligning with the interests of everyone. See much more about rules and how to created and apply them in Chapter 10.

Classroom rituals are another important piece of creating a culture of caring. All cultures have rituals that help define them. Rituals that help distinguish classroom communities include special ways that students and teachers interact, special ways that everyone celebrates the successes of others, and special ways that challenges to the ethics that drive the classroom are handled. One kind of ritual that many teachers employ to further the aims of a caring community of learners is classroom meetings (Edwards, 2003; Styles, 2001). Classroom meetings are structured events that follow a prescribed format. According to Styles (2001),

[They] provide students with the opportunity to participate in a group exchange of ideas in a respectful, caring atmosphere. [They] are a place to share, encourage, listen, think, decide, plan, and evaluate. (p. 7)

Holding regular classroom meetings signals students that everyone's voice is valued, that sharing feelings and ideas in a safe space is important, and that we can work together to solve problems.

Rituals of celebration are important elements of culture. In classrooms, celebrating the personal, social, and academic successes of peers, helps students and teachers connect and reinforces their feelings of confidence. When I taught in elementary classrooms, we set aside time at the end of the school day to reflect on what we had accomplished as individuals and as a group. Upper grade students can do the same at the end of class periods.

Another way to bolster the stability of classroom communities is to have rituals in place for addressing disruptions that arise. Here is the place for making direct reference to the rules that are in place to maximize the group's chances of accomplishing its shared purpose. It is not the teacher losing her or his patience and docking student points, making kids move their cards, or sending kids to time-out or suspension. It is about saying something like, "We have a rule that you cannot do things that hurt other students' chances of learning. When you _____, we cannot learn _____. What do you need to do to make sure we can all learn?" It is a ritual because it is predictable, it is based on the shared ethos of the class, and it gives rule breakers the chance to maintain their full status as group members.

Most young people do not show up with all the necessary skills and attitudes to be productive members of a classroom community. They need to learn and practice the routines and rituals that define a caring community of learners, and they need to hone basic social skills that are vital to operating in this special kind of environment (Levine, 2003). Examples of important social skills include communicating (listening and responding), working together, making decisions, asking for help, ignoring distractions, and problem solving (Levine, 2003; National Association of School Psychologists, 2002). Learning and practicing social skills are not an annoyance that gets in the way of academic achievement; they represent a set of dispositions and behaviors that are central to success in school and life.

Teachers can improve the social capacities of their students by taking time to systematically teach social skills, then giving students lots of opportunities for practice and feedback. Teaching social skills means giving students concrete sets of behaviors that can be applied in specific situations. For example, the teacher might ask students to name behaviors that demonstrate what listening looks like (e.g., eye contact, nodding, body language, restating, asking for clarification), then generate a list of descriptors of what listening does not look like (e.g., talking over, talking to others, turning away, ignoring). Students then might be asked to role-play scenarios in which listening behaviors are contrasted with non-listening behaviors, followed by a discussion of how people feel when they know they are (or are not) being listened to. Social skills lessons are seldom one-and-done activities. They need to be reinforced frequently, especially as specific needs arise. The overall message should be: "We are in this together, so we need to be as socially smart as we can be."

Caring communities of learning do not trade the caring part for the learning part. Academic learning does not take a back seat in these settings. The school curriculum is in place, and good teachers make wise decisions about how to implement it. It is the "how" of teaching in a classroom community that makes all the difference. The essence of the difference is the mutual engagement of everyone in everyone else's success. Achievement is advanced in classrooms where there is a shared purpose and a network of support in place. When everyone is invested in the success of everyone else, then each individual's chances for academic advancement are improved.

Looking back at my teaching career, I cannot say I was always successful at setting my classrooms up as learning communities. It is my nature to be critical of myself, and that is a good and a bad thing. It is good to accept and reflect on your mistakes—that is how you get better; but it can be bad if you let an obsession with screw-ups overshadow the positive things you have done.

Most of the disappointments I feel when I think back across my teaching career are tied to times when I did or said something stupid, immature, or hurtful in reaction to a specific situation. In the context or creating a caring community of learners, these were times that jeopardized the human connections at the core of this concept. I still experience a sinking feeling inside when I recall times when I blew it and said something to student that made him or her feel like I did not care—like I could not be trusted to be a mature role-model, guide and mentor.

Still, even in times when I let myself and my students down, I kept trying. I tried to come clean about my mistakes, to apologize, and to explain how I would try to do better. Even when I felt overwhelmed and frustrated with my inability to create the kind of classroom culture described here (see Chapter 19 about avoiding power struggles), I kept trying. Classrooms are populated by humans, and humans err. Students and teachers err. Acknowledging your humanness and your capacity to make mistakes can be part of creating a caring community of learners. Do not forget to extend the same grace to your students.

This chapter has provided a sketch of why doing everything you can to make your classroom a caring community of learners is important and given some guidance about how to go about it. This book is an overall guide to building classroom cultures that bring to life the human connections that distinguish caring classrooms from those that are sterile, robotic, and joyless. Like me, you will never be perfect. You will miss opportunities and make mistakes, but you can learn from your mistakes and make sure to take advantages of opportunities the next time they present themselves.

What you must not do is become inured to school life, no matter how tough it may seem at times. You must not become one of the teachers you have observed who goes through the motions of teaching, treating students as an annoyance and watching the clock so they can be the first one out of the parking lot. I worry because I cannot believe that those teachers started their careers with a dispassionate attitude—they must have felt some of the same feelings of commitment and caring that brought you and me to teaching. So I worry that if it happened to them, it could happen to you.

You cannot let yourself become anything less than the best teacher you can be. Later chapters in this book give lots of advice for being reflective, monitoring your own socialization into the profession, and avoiding burnout. Setting up classrooms as learning communities provides a structure on which to build the human connections that make teaching meaningful, powerful, and fulfilling. It is not magic; but it is an invaluable tool for ensuring that you stay connected to your students and fulfill your purpose for being there.

REFERENCES

Edwards, D. (2003). Classroom meetings: Encouraging a climate of cooperation. *Professional School Counseling, 7*(1), 20–28.

Levine, D. A. (2003). *Building classroom communities: Strategies for developing a culture of caring.* Solution Tree Press.

National Association of School Psychologists. (2002). *Social skills: Promoting positive behavior, academic success, and school safety.* NASP Fact Sheet. https://www.nasp-center.org/factsheets/socialskills_fs.html

Noddings, N. (1995). Teaching themes of care. *Phi Delta Kappan, 76*(9), 675–679.

Noddings, N. (2013). *Caring: A relational approach to ethics and moral education.* University of California Press.

Styles, D. (2001). *Class meetings: Building leadership, problem solving and decision making skills in the respectful classroom.* Pembroke.

CHAPTER 4

IT IS SHORTSIGHTED TO THINK THAT HAVING FUN IS A WORTHY GOAL FOR CLASSROOM ACTIVITY

I am pretty serious by nature. I am awkwardly shy and withdrawn in social settings that require me to interact with folks I do not know well. I doubt that someone would describe me as a "fun guy." But that does not mean I do not think having fun is an important part of life or that I do not seek out fun activities with people I like. I cut my teaching teeth in elementary school classrooms and lots of the things we did produced feelings of fun as a byproduct. However, even as a novice second grade teacher, I was never convinced my job was to provide fun activities for my students, and I never tried to con my students into putting forth effort because a particular activity was going to be "fun." This chapter is about countering the narrative that school should be or has to be fun in order to get students interested and engaged. I told you I am no fun guy.

At the same time I was teaching second grade in Jacksonville, Florida, I had a girlfriend (also a teacher) who had a completely different worldview regarding the place of fun in and out of school. We recognized and even joked about the differences in our worldviews. I would argue that life is a series of challenges to be overcome and that satisfaction comes from facing down the inevitable obstacles that come our way. Becky (not her real name) mocked me as a hopeless pessimist, averring that life was made up

Teaching as a Human Activity: Ways to Make Classrooms Joyful and Effective
pp. 27–34

of opportunities for having fun, and having a rich life meant taking advantage of as many of those opportunities as possible. Becky and I had a great couple of on-again-off-again years together—lots of heartache and lots of fun.

Becky and I fell apart for good when I developed blood clots in my lungs as a result of a minor arm injury that I incurred playing in a softball tournament. I was in intensive care for 10 days and in recovery for another 10. Becky was put out by my injury—not because my life was in danger, but because it got in the way of lots of early summer opportunities to have fun. She seemed annoyed that she had to visit and ultimately stopped coming to the hospital at all. This was the days before cell phones, so she was unreachable by landline day and night. She was out having fun.

But this is a book about teaching, not good love gone bad. Becky's focus on fun extended to her teaching. She was a terrific, energetic, fun teacher—the kind lots of kids remember as a favorite. She was unapologetic about her approach. Her students had fun and so did she, and I am sure her students learned a great deal from her. Naturally, our views on the place of fun in school were polar opposites. She saw fun as her *modus operandi* and learning as the natural byproduct; for me, learning should be what we are all about and fun might be (or not) a secondary outcome of the learning process.

So the thesis of this chapter is that it is great if a sense of fun is a side benefit of some learning-filled school experiences; but having fun is a vapid goal in and of itself. In fact, I believe we should be teaching students that learning is often hard; and because it is hard, accomplishing it is satisfying and gratifying in ways that go beyond a transitory feeling of having fun.

I do not want to wander too far afield by taking a side trip into some arcane theory from your Intro to Philosophical class; but at some level, I am arguing here that fun is not an inherent good. Remember reading Jeremy Bentham (1789) and John Stuart Mill (1879) on utilitarianism? These great thinkers made the case that happiness is the only intrinsic good. There are lots of other experiences that have instrumental (secondary) value, but pleasure and freedom from pain are the only inherently desirable ends of human activity. Becky was no moral philosopher, but her view of the importance of maximizing fun as the ultimate aim of life was not wildly misplaced. It sounds unfair to call her a hedonist because of the contemporary salacious view of that term; but in the minds of the early utilitarians, her focus on fun would be called hedonistic.

As will be evident in Chapter 9, John Rawls (1971) is my favorite philosopher. His emphasis on self-respect as the most important primary good and justice as a moral imperative seems more on target than arguing for pleasure seeking as the ultimate human aim. Without protracting this side journey, I am not sure that fun (or pleasure) is the only or ultimate good. Surely, there are other candidates like kindness, self-respect, accomplishment, or love. Further, you could argue that not all pleasure is even valuable at all. It is possible to have fun in ways that hurt others or yourself. In the classroom, it is possible that treating fun as the ultimate good could cast a negative shadow over other aims that are much more worthy. It is possible that an obsession with having fun could teach children to think that anything that is not fun is not worth doing.

As should be clear from the previous chapters, I believe expending genuine effort in the name of a worthy goal should be expected, recognized and celebrated in classrooms. If we want school to be a place where meaningful activity dominates, teachers have to help students see that the learning process requires work that can lead to satisfaction, even when it is not always fun. This chapter discusses the value of reframing our approach to motivating students and provides examples of approaches and activities that help students experience the pride and self-fulfillment that accompany the accomplishment of difficult tasks that have meaning to their lives.

It is a trap to try to sell schooling as fun. It is even risky to tell students that they are about to participate in a fun activity (almost a bad as saying it will be easy). Establishing the expectation that school itself or specific activities in school are fun sets a standard that is as hard to meet as it is hard to defend. If every activity or selected activities do not satisfy the fun quotient, then teachers can "fail" even when they have provided experiences that enrich students' lives—academic and otherwise. Overpromising fun in school sets teachers up for sacrificing rigor for entertainment, swapping learning for amusement, and trading education for enjoyment. Others may see the possibility of covering the entire prescribed curriculum in fun ways, but expecting yourself to accomplish that lofty goal sets you up for a fall. I think it is too heavy a lift in terms of time and energy. Worse, it is an near-impossible ask—kids' ideas of what counts as fun may look nothing like what you had in mind.

Part of the subtext of promoting fun as a legitimate purpose of school turns out to be, "If it is not fun, it is not worth doing." Children and young people who expect to be entertained in school think they can reasonably object when asked to take on assignments that they do not perceive as fun. I have observed some teachers (even teachers I admire) take the stance that, "If it were up to me, all the activities we do would be fun; but _____ (fill in 'the system,' 'the superintendent,' 'the people who make the tests,' 'teachers at the next grade level,' or someone else) makes us do this hard work too." It is classic role distancing, as in: "It is part of my job to teach you this, even though I would never do it by choice." I understand the feelings behind this line of thinking; but to me it is a cop–out. You do not have to find excuses or identify scapegoats for not providing fun activities for your students. You just need to drop the façade that school should be all fun all the time.

Another familiar tune that I hear teachers singing goes something like, "Kids today are used to high-tech stimulation and the immediate gratification they get from video games, TV, computers, and cell phones! How am I supposed to compete with that?" My short answer is, "You are not." But, this is more complex than merely dropping the pretense that school is going to be fun. There is serious scholarship suggesting that the ways that children and young people process information and how their senses and brains work may be changing because of so much exposure to screen-based technological advances (e.g., Postman, 1985; Rudder, 2019). It is clear that there are genuinely positive ways teachers can integrate technology into their classrooms (see Chapter 16). But we lose if we set ourselves up as competitors with advanced technologies for the attention of our students. For me, the substance and the human contact are what count.

If learning can be enriched, accelerated or improved using technology, then I am all for it. But, no technological innovation can ever replace the impact one caring human has on another. What teachers have to offer might be supplemented by cool websites or interactive cell phone apps, but what we bring can never be supplanted electronically. As I have emphasized throughout this book, it is the human connections that make learning meaningful and worth pursuing. Thinking that we have to compete with the electronic media that saturate our students' experience out of class is a dead-end street. It is much wiser to take the stance that we have a good reason for being here and for working together, so we are going to use all of our human and technological resources to accomplish our aims. Technology needs to be framed as a useful tool for making our lives as rich and rewarding as possible—not as an end in and of itself (like some kind of cyber inherent good).

We do not have to trick kids into getting satisfaction from schooling, acting as if learning has to be disguised as a game (video or otherwise) to make it worth doing. I hope I have made my point that it is a doomed strategy to try to make fun the object of your lessons. Not only will the students see right through the masquerade, they will play you when the inevitable cracks in your façade appear, as in: "Why do we have to do all this boring stuff? Why can't we work on our tablets some more?" Better to establish an ethos of shared learning in the classroom and frame it as hard, satisfying, fulfilling work.

I remember speaking to a group of parents about helping their children be successful in school. In my prepared remarks, I tried to make the point that their children were learning what the parents thought about school and learning from what they said and did around their kids. I was trying to help them see how their attitudes about school and school tasks would rub off on their kids. I made a special example of how the ways they approached reading and books sent powerful messages to their children, encouraging them to let their children see them using and enjoying books and especially reading with their children to show how mature readers operate on and value text.

Near the end of the question and answer session that followed my talk, one mother asked, "But what do I do if I do not like reading myself? I have always hated to read, and I read as little as possible to this day." I remember being caught off guard by this question, and I am still not sure there is a good answer. Best I could come up with on the spot was pretty lame: "If you want your child to love reading, then you should pretend that you love it too." It is not much better, but I might have said, "It is okay to tell your daughter the truth about your feelings about reading, but also tell her how much you hope she learns to love reading and how important it is to be a good reader."

So, I am trying to imagine what you are thinking as you read this story and this chapter. I want you to reflect on how you think of yourself in relation to learning, to analyze the (often hidden) messages you send or will send your students when you present school tasks to them. What if you have feelings about school (or reading) that parallel those of the mother in the Q and A session? What if your experience in school was not one you would characterize as being part of a community of learners? Can you still create classroom communities in which everyone shares a commitment to everyone else's success, even when success is often hard earned? I hope so!

I have worked with hundreds of new and future teachers. A large number were brilliant additions to the teaching profession, and almost all were prepared to make strong positive contributions to the lives of young people. A few, one or two a year, were not good fits for teaching. I recall one young woman who was struggling during the yearlong internship required in our teacher education program at the University of Tennessee. When asked in postobservation sessions with her university supervisor to critique her teaching during the lesson, she always thought she was perfect. Worse, she resented that her mentor found places where she needed to improve. This pattern escalated to the point where a meeting of her professors and field-experience supervisors had to be called. When we advised that she needed to be more reflective about her teaching and to think more deeply about how to improve, she stubbornly replied, "I don't do deep."

So, can you create a classroom in which everyone shares the belief that learning is hard but worth it, even if you are not so sure yourself? I think you can, but not unless you are willing and able to "do deep." In fact, I am just fine with your choosing to take a route completely different from the ones suggested in this book (even if it is a journey aimed at having fun in the classroom). The caveat is you need to be deeply thoughtful about where you want to go and how you want to get there. In lots of schools and too many classrooms, teachers and students (and everyone involved) operate in an environment void of purpose. You can change that in your classroom. You can think through what you value and develop strategies to imbed those values in your actions and invite your students join you in making those values come to life. Some specific examples of how this has been done follow.

Mariana Souto-Manning is one of my favorite people in education. She is a professor at Teachers College, Columbia University, and she was a successful and innovative teacher in Brazil and the United States before entering academia. She has used what she learned teaching preschool through graduate school to help other teachers use culture circles to implement critical pedagogy approaches in their classrooms (Souto-Manning, 2010). Utilizing culture circles is one example of an approach that can give meaning and purpose to what goes on in classrooms—one way that you could help students see that hard work can have big payoffs.

Culture circles are based on the work of Mariana's Brazilian country-man, Paulo Freire (1970), who argued that teaching should not be a process of transferring information from adults to children (what Freire called a banking concept of education). Instead, education should be an interactive process that takes into account the cultural knowledge and experience that students bring to school. Knowledge is thought to be historically and socially situated, and students and their teachers use culture circles to pose problems, engage in critical dialogue, solve problems, and take action (Souto-Manning, 2010). You can imagine how different the experience would look and feel for students who see their role in school to be critical readers of the world, rather than passive recipients of the prescribed curriculum.

A study done in high schools in California offers an example of how culture circles were implemented in secondary classrooms. A. Dee Williams (2009) studied classroom culture circles led by an English teacher, which were built around the lived experiences of students with a focus on hip-hop culture. Lectures were eliminated, and students took on learning units as participants in dialogic interactions to clarify shared understandings and decide on actions. The aims of the program were to support the students as they developed (a) their use of "counter narratives;" (b) a "language of critique and transcendence;" and (c) "the awakening of a critical awareness" (Williams, 2009, p. 6).

The student participants developed their skills through an analysis of hip-hop culture, starting with the question: "What problems do you see in hip-hop today?" (p. 13). This framework led the students to complex analyses of issues related to hip-hop, including misogyny, violence and drugs; keeping it real once artists are successful; and outside influences and commercial control. Coming out of their dialogic discussions, students were encouraged to generate solutions and take action based on the knowledge they had constructed together.

A study of K–12 classrooms in Ohio offers an additional example how an alternative set of educational purposes can lead to activities and learning that provide students and teachers with reasons for being engaged and working hard, even when it might not be fun. In the classrooms described by Collins et al. (2019), the focus was on how teachers establish and maintain the use of democratic principles and processes in their classrooms. Teachers in the study applied concepts of democratic education described by John Dewey (1916), who argued that one of the school's primary functions was to create active, engaged, critically thinking members of society.

Collins and colleagues (2019) noted that teachers in their study not only taught students about how democracy as a political system is supposed to work, they structured their classrooms so that democratic principles were applied and students learned first-hand how to operate in democratic settings. Key features that the teachers noted as necessary for democratic education to succeed included: fostering relationships, empowering students, teaching and using democratic skills, and creating a democratic educative structure. This study shows that a thoughtfully constructed educational purpose like creating classroom democracies can be implemented across the grade spectrum in public schools.

As you "do deep" and think hard about yourself as a teacher, I hope you will take on a basic philosophical question and then reflect on what your answer might mean for your teaching. The question is: What do you count as an inherent good? Tough question—one that great minds have struggled with for centuries. Maybe you see yourself as a classic utilitarian and believe pleasure is the ultimate good. Maybe you align more closely with pragmatists like Dewey and believe that living by democratic principles is central to a fulfilling life. Maybe you can list several worthy aims for having a full rich life. Your answer does not matter so much as the process of thinking it through then reflecting on what it means for your classroom.

Almost everyone thinks they can teach. Lay people have seen teaching for 12 or more years and figure they could do it without any special preparation (Hatch, 2005). We know differently. Real teachers understand the vast array of knowledge, skills, and dispositions required to be effective in the classroom. I am arguing here and throughout this book that a critical difference that real teachers bring to their work is a reflective stance on what they are doing and why. If you know what you value as a human being and you can translate that into your practice, you will indeed be a reflective professional practitioner. If you believe in what you are doing and do your best to act on your beliefs, your students, the adults who care for them, and your peers and supervisors will recognize and respect your efforts. Best of all, you will be able to look at yourself in the mirror as you drive home and say, "I did some important work today!"

REFERENCES

Bentham, J. (1789). *An introduction to the principles of morals and legislation.* Clarendon Press.

Collins, S., Hess, M. E., & Lowery, C. L. (2019). Democratic spaces: How teachers establish and sustain democracy and education in their classrooms. *Democracy & Education, 27*(1), 1–11.

Dewey, J. (1916). *Democracy and education.* Macmillan.

Freire, P. (1970). *Pedagogy of the oppressed.* Continuum.

Mill, J. S. (1879). *Utilitarianism.* Longmans, Green, and Company.

Hatch, J. A. (2005). Why America needs to hate its public schools. *Principal, 85,* 69–70.

Postman, N. (1985). *Amusing ourselves to death: Public discourse in the age of show business.* Penguin.

Rawls, J. (1971). *A theory of justice.* Harvard University Press.

Rudder, D. B. (2019, June 19). *Screen time and the brain.* Harvard Medical School. https://hms.harvard.edu/news/screen-time-brain

Souto-Manning, M. (2010). *Freire, teaching, and learning: Culture circles across contexts.* Peter Lang.

Williams, A. D. (2009). The critical cultural cypher: Remaking Paulo Freire's cultural circles using Hip Hop culture. *International Journal of Critical Pedagogy, 2*(1) 1–29.

PART II

**HOW CAN I MAKE MY TEACHING EFFECTIVE
BY BUILDING ON VITAL HUMAN CONNECTIONS
WITH MY STUDENTS?**

CHAPTER 5

TEACHING THAT IGNORES THE HUMANNESS OF STUDENTS AND TEACHERS IS JOYLESS AND LIMITED IN EFFECTIVENESS

Teaching as a Human Activity was chosen for the main title of this book because I wanted to provide a counter narrative to what seems to be happening a lot in today's schools. Seems to me that we are drifting away from our humanity in the ways we structure, administer, and evaluate schooling. I do not say this to slam teachers. My experience tells me teachers come to education as a field of endeavor because of the most human of reasons: They want to touch the lives of children and young people. Most do their best to hold fast to their goal of making a difference for children and society; but over time, it has become more difficult for teachers to express in classrooms what they feel in their heart of hearts. I hope this chapter and this book provide inspiration and specific strategies that teachers can use to make their teaching more human, more satisfying, and more effective.

I have written extensively about what has gone wrong with public education over the past decades (e.g., Hatch, 2002, 2005, 2007, 2015). I do not want to flog that horse here, but I will provide a quick overview of factors that I think inhibit the expression of humanity in both students and

Teaching as a Human Activity: Ways to Make Classrooms Joyful and Effective
pp. 37–44
Copyright © 2021 by Information Age Publishing
37

teachers. What I want to emphasize is that teachers have the opportunity to touch their students' lives in profoundly human ways, even when they work in systems that limit and sometimes discourage them from doing so.

A few years back, one of the reviewers of a proposal I prepared for another book for teachers was put off by what he or she thought was the negative tone of the book, arguing that new and future teachers should not be exposed to the problems associated with working in schools because it might discourage them as they enter the profession. That sounds a little patronizing and a lot dishonest to me. It seems way smarter to let novice teachers know about the realities of the work life they are beginning and give them tools for adjusting to those realities than to pretend that the field of education is a bed of roses, without any thorns at all.

The preservice teachers with whom I have worked have been smart, savvy people who know bullshit when they hear it. They can handle the truth so long as you provide tools for them to overcome the obstacles to their becoming successful, self-fulfilled, contributing teachers. What then are some of the factors that mitigate the chances of being fully human in contemporary classrooms? Once those are laid out, we will look at tools for overcoming those obstacles.

It is hard to separate some of the forces working against expressing humanity in schools from each other or to figure out what might be causing what. For sure, the notion of educational *accountability* is related to other factors to be discussed and it is the root cause for at least some. The accountability movement has been around since the publication of *A Nation at Risk* in the 1980s (National Commission on Excellence in Education, 1983). The premise of this influential document and of the arguments that have persisted since then is that educators cannot be trusted to prepare America's youth to be productive members of society, so outside forces need to be applied to hold them accountable (Berliner & Biddle, 1995; Hatch, 2015). Those outside forces want to crack the whip and get teachers in line. They have little (no?) interest in making humanity a vital part of the school experience for teachers or students.

Standards-based testing is how the system has chosen to ensure accountability. Again, the assumption was that schools had no standards and no valid way to assess what they were doing. So, consultants and testing companies were hired to develop standards on which teaching needed to be focused and to create standardized assessment instruments to evaluate how well the standards were being met. Textbook companies changed their business model to match the standards-based approach and began producing materials based on state standards and marketing them as tools for preparing students to pass tests. Now, it is almost impossible to think of public schooling without standardized testing, and it is dizzying to consider the impact this movement has had on teaching and learning

(Hatch, 2007). Although there is occasional resistance from within and outside of education (e.g., Darling-Hammond, 2004; Strauss, 2014), I do not believe standards or testing will go away. However, I know there is room for a more human approach to doing school than just capitulating to the standards-based testing regime.

The application of *business models* to schooling is another pervasive feature that devalues the expression of humanness in classrooms. Of course, this phenomenon goes hand in hand with accountability and standards-based assessment. Powerful people from the business world and their political cronies have convinced the American public that, left to their own devices, educators lack efficiency, effectiveness, and motivation. Critics want to reform schools so that they are run like businesses; in fact, many want to privatize schooling, taking public education out of the hands of education professionals and delivering it to entrepreneurs and for-profit corporations (Hatch, 2015; Ravitch, 2013). Powerful business moguls, super-rich philanthropists, and opportunistic politicians see schools as easy targets for applying market-based principles, but they have no idea what goes on in real classrooms (Berliner & Glass, 2014; Hatch, 2015). People like us who actually know what children and young adults are like and what they need must take advantage of our opportunities to make a positive difference every day with every student.

Teacher deprofessionalization is an outcome of the factors described so far. One of my saddest realizations as an educator is that teacher autonomy has dramatically eroded over my 45-plus years in the field. When I started, teachers had curriculum guides to refer to and textbooks to support them; but they decided what would be taught, how it would be taught, and how their students' learning would be assessed. As we have seen above, *what will be taught* is now reduced to sets of standards that dominate virtually all of the instructional time available, and the *how it will be assessed* is determined by mandatory testing regimens. Defenders of the standards-based accountability movement sometimes claim that teachers can still decide *how they will teach;* but my experience and the testimony of the many teachers I know is that curriculum developers, textbook companies, and programs adopted by many schools mostly prescribe how and when teaching is supposed to happen. As a teacher educator, my stance was always to prepare professional decision makers, with special knowledge, skills, and dispositions that lay people just do not have. With that privileged positionality comes big responsibility. Working in the current deprofessionalizing climate of schools magnifies that responsibility even more.

A general *lack of respect for teachers* follows from and somehow justifies the obsession with holding teachers accountable, depending on standardized testing to assess the value of schooling, applying business models in educational institutions, and taking away teacher autonomy. In the perception of politicians, the press, and the general public, schools are populated by teachers who teach because there is little else they are qualified to do; they come from the shallow end of college student pool; and they deserve the low pay they receive compared to others with similar training. I have argued elsewhere (Hatch, 2005, 2015) that schools are easy targets for derision because everyone who has spent time in schools thinks he or she knows as much about teaching as a trained professional. Further, as public employees, teachers cannot fight back. If they raise their voices in protest or support the legitimate aims of their unions, they are labeled as selfish and uncaring. So, if these factors are part of the contemporary education milieu, what can teachers do to be sure they bring their humanity to bear on what happens every day in school?

I want to be clear that I think teacher activism is important. I have added my voice to many others who have called for teachers to stand up to powerful outsiders who want to reform education to satisfy their own political and economic ends (e.g., Hatch, 2015; Kumishiro, 2012; Schniedewind & Sapon-Shevin, 2012). But this chapter and this book are about making classroom experiences more human, finding ways to live out what really matters. The remainder of this chapter will focus on working around the negative forces described above so that you and your students can leave school each day feeling like something important happened because we were able to acknowledge and express our humanity.

For starters, let's set up classrooms so that everyone is accountable for the growth and development of everyone else. Accountability is not inherently bad. Doing what is right is a basic human responsibility, and making yourself accountable for your actions is central to being a fully functioning person. As individual teachers, we can stake out our territory by proclaiming that we will be accountable to our selves, our students, our profession, and our communities. We will do our best to apply our professional knowledge and skill to improve the life chances of those we serve. We will establish a culture of shared responsibility in our classrooms and live out our commitment to helping *each* student support the learning and development of *every* student. In other fields, professionals hold themselves accountable. Physicians, lawyers, or engineers do not let outside forces set standards or decide who is meeting them or not. While teachers will likely have to live with accountability expectations imposed by more powerful others, we do not have to let them define who we are, tell us why we are there, or stipulate everything we do.

Let's not pretend that scores on standardized tests measure our students' worth as people or our value as teachers. Test scores tell us something; but they mask far more than they reveal. A few of the issues that make experts wary of using standards-based testing to assess student learning and teacher proficiency include the following (from Hatch, 2015, pp. 31–33):

- Standardized tests are constructed in ways that advantage certain groups and disadvantage others;
- Standardized test scores cannot represent the complexity of the teaching and learning process;
- Standardized tests are incomplete measures of educational outcomes;
- Standardized tests underestimate the effects of out-of-school factors on student performance;
- Timed portions of standardized tests may distort what students actually know and are capable of doing;
- Standardized tests include measurement error that is often ignored as results are reported;
- Standardized tests are often ill matched to the standards and curricula the schools are teaching.

For a long time, I taught that the teaching and learning process could be captured in the image of the three-legged stool, with curriculum, instruction, and assessment representing the three legs. In this model, assessment is an integral part of the process because it provides a feedback loop that lets students know where they stand and informs teachers' decisions about future curriculum and instruction. In this approach, assessment means asking students to demonstrate that they have learned what was just taught. They see that getting feedback is a natural and logical step in their learning. Obviously, the high-stakes testing that dominates assessment practices in contemporary schools distorts the image of the three-legged stool beyond recognition. Again, standardized testing may not go away any time soon, but we can show our students that we value their learning by utilizing meaningful assessment strategies that make perfect sense and never need not be sterile, unfair, or "high stakes."

Let's proclaim that person-to-person relationships are critical to the teaching learning process. Meaningful schooling for humans can never be about inputs and outputs. Business models will never work for education because children are not raw materials that can be molded into particular products by applying standardized procedures along an assembly line. Kids are not widgets and teachers are not robots. Every student brings a unique set of experiences, talents, and challenges to the classroom. Teachers bring their own backgrounds, strengths, and shortcomings. Instead of pretending we can wash out the complexity of human learning by making schools like factories, let us celebrate our innate capacities to mutually impact each other's lives. Let's acknowledge that social interactions are the stuff of a fully human existence. Let's talk more about building healthy relationships in school and less about privatization and improving the bottom line. Let's be sure we talk about nurturing healthy human relationships as the best way to improve student learning. We cannot win if we let our critics trap us with their tired argument that we want schools to be "warm and fuzzy" environments void of rigor or hard work. The whole point of this book is that learning is fulfilling because it is hard, and rigor is welcome because it leads to self-respect. We can win if we help others understand that the learning we nurture in our students is enriched and enlivened when we engage with them in making classrooms places where human complexity is recognized and honored. We can meet the expectations of the systems within which we work without denying our responsibility to do what is right for the young human beings we serve.

Let's demonstrate our professionalism every day. In a world that seems to value technocratic approaches that deprofessionalize teaching, let's show everyone that we have specialized understandings and commitments that make us capable of making decisions no one else is qualified to make. For starters, we need to unmask the charade that the young people in our care are one-dimensional creatures whose job in school is to master a narrowly defined set of skills and concepts. As professionals, we know that cognitive development is much broader than the scope and sequences that dominate classroom instruction in the current model. Further, we know that you cannot separate cognitive growth from other aspects of human development, especially social, emotional, physical, and language development. There is no program, technology, or AI application that can process the information and make the decisions necessary to meet the needs of a classroom full of young humans. Attempting to deprofessionalize teaching is an insult; but it's also stupid. We have to show what we are worth by demonstrating how powerfully we can impact schools and society when we utilize our specialized knowledge and apply our professional commitments to make our classrooms dynamic, exciting places where children learn, develop, and thrive.

Let's have a "rap" to express our pride in what we do—to our students, colleagues, friends, and family. Not long after the second edition was published, I invited Bill Ayers to campus to talk about his powerful manifesto: *To Teach* (Ayers, 2001). One of the most memorable things he told the new and future teachers in the audience was that we should be ready on every occasion to talk about how proud we are to be doing the important work of teaching. Bill's experience matched my own when he pointed out that school folks often answer the "What do you do?" question at social gatherings with, "I'm just a teacher" (or self-effacing words to that effect). Professor Ayers said we should all have a "rap" (a prepared speech, not a freestyle hip-hop poem) at the ready and use it to convince others that we know how important our work is and we know that we are good at it—something like: "I have the best job ever. I get to use all I know about teaching and learning to impact the future of the world. What do you do?" Along with speaking up for ourselves, we need to support other teachers. Sometimes, we fall into the trap of believing the propaganda that school reformers lay out to demean teachers (Hatch, 2015; Kumishiro, 2012), so we respond to our critics by offering that, "Teachers at my school are fine" or "My system is good," while throwing other educators and schools under the bus. Let's be proud of ourselves and each other and stop being afraid to let others know that we are professionals who deserve their respect.

Of course, I am hoping that this book is not a cry in the wilderness. I want to help teachers see the primal value of bringing humanness to the forefront of what we do, and I want them fight hard to make that happen. I am part of a book club comprised of retired folks from a variety of occupational backgrounds. Each month, we read, then discuss, a current nonfiction book that appears to be important. By chance, the book we are reading as I write this chapter is all about megatrends that will shape the future, and it includes a section arguing that returning to a "human mode" is 1 of 10 megatrends to be reckoned with (Bhargava, 2020). The author makes the case that, "In a world booming with technology, there are signs that our humanity matters more than ever before" (p. 114) and that "Sometimes the best innovation is to focus on improving the humanity of an experience rather than making it faster or cheaper" (p. 120). If the careful analyses behind this book's projections are right, then making classrooms more human might fit right in with a larger movement to bring more humanity to all aspects of life. Either way, ignoring the humanness of students and teachers makes classrooms into joyless places and limits everyone's chances of experiencing invaluable connections with content, meaning, and other people.

REFERENCES

Ayers, W. (2001). *To teach: The journey of a teacher* (2nd ed.). Teachers College Press.

Berliner, D. C., & Biddle, B. J. (1995). *The manufactured crisis: Myths, fraud, and the attack on America's public schools.* Basic Books.

Berliner, D. C., & Glass, G. V. (2014). *50 myths and lies that threaten America's public schools: The real crisis in education.* Teachers College Press.

Bhargava, R. (2020). *Non-obvious megatrends.* Ideapress.

Darling-Hammond, L. (2004). Standards, accountability, and school reform. *Teachers College Record, 106,* 1047–1085.

Hatch, J. A. (2002). Accountability shovedown: Resisting the standards movement in early childhood education. *Phi Delta Kappan, 83,* 457-462.

Hatch, J. A. (2005). Why America needs to hate its public schools. *Principal, 85,* 69-70.

Hatch, J. A. (2007). Learning as a subversive activity. *Phi Delta Kappan, 89,* 310-311.

Hatch, J. A. (2015). *Reclaiming the teaching profession: Transforming the dialogue on public education.* Rowman & Littlefield.

Kumishiro, K. K. (2012). *Bad teacher: How blaming teachers distorts the bigger picture.* Teachers College Press.

National Commission on Excellence in Education. (1983). *A nation at risk: The imperative for educational reform.* United States Department of Education.

Schniedewind, N., & Sapon-Shevin, M. (Eds.). (2012). *Educational courage: Resisting the ambush of public education.* Beacon Press.

Strauss, V. (2014, July 10). What 4 teachers told Obama over lunch. *Washington Post.* https://ed311.com/what-4-teachers-told-obama-over-lunch/

CHAPTER 6

STUDENTS NEED TO SEE LEARNING AS AN INHERENTLY VALUABLE HUMAN ACTIVITY AND THAT THEY ARE FULLY CAPABLE LEARNERS

Early in my career as an elementary teacher, I had the amazing opportunity to design and implement a program intended to help primary-age kids who did not qualify for special education services but who were considered to be "at risk" for school failure. My class was a mixed-age, mixed-race class of first, second, and third grade students in a Title I school that had been recently desegregated in Jacksonville, Florida. What made it amazing was that I was given full responsibility for building the curriculum and deciding on the teaching strategies. No scripted lessons, canned curricula, or prescribed computer programs—it was up to me to figure out what each child needed in order to be successful.

I learned a ton about children, teaching, and myself during the two years I worked in that program. What I learned most about was the notion of learning itself. When I was depending on others to tell me what to teach, how to teach, and when to teach, I did not really stop to think about what was going on as students interacted (or not) with the activities I was implementing day to day. Starting from scratch with this terrific group of kids forced me to examine the learning process in ways I had not

Teaching as a Human Activity: Ways to Make Classrooms Joyful and Effective
pp. 45–53
Copyright © 2021 by Information Age Publishing

done before; and that experience changed my life as a teacher and as a human being.

It was not like I had this stunning "aha!" moment when I suddenly figured everything out. My insight was embedded in reflections on the multitude of daily interactions I had with these primary-age children. Early on I realized that these kids did not see themselves as competent learners. The system had already told them that they were less than normal, and they had internalized the stigma that goes with being labeled "at risk" (Swadener & Lubeck, 1995). Believing that they could not do school stuff, many of them shut down because it is easier to play off your perceived inadequacies if you do not try. Others' ways of coping were more defiant, as in, "You cannot make me do this crap!"

I figured I had to break through somehow and show them that they were capable of learning. In the process of trying to find ways to do that, I realized a fundamental and troubling truth: they had no idea what real learning is all about. Yes, they had filled in hundreds of blanks on workbook pages, sat through scores of math lessons, and recited innumerous answers during reading group time; but no one had ever taught them what learning is, what it looks like, how it feels, or how to do it.

Over the years, I have come to see this lack of understanding of what human learning is all about to be a problem that impacts the lives of too many children in school. It was not just these young kids with a record of struggling in school who did not know what learning is; it seems to me lots of students across the education spectrum find school difficult and even punishing because they have not learned how to learn or to think of themselves as competent learners. Part of the problem is that many schools have become so preoccupied with standards, testing, and test preparation that genuine learning and the joy inherent in being a learner have been pushed to the side. It is a sad thought, but many students can get through their educational careers (including college for some) and never know the ecstasy of experiencing themselves as competent, confident learners.

Yes, I used the word *ecstasy*. The kind of learning I am talking about is comprised of cognitive and affective processes that go on in humans and no other animals. Being able to learn to do important things that we could not previously do or understand important notions we could not previously understand makes humans unique. In fact, our capacity to use our brains to learn new skills and comprehend new information helps define our humanness (Choi, 2016). *Homo sapiens* means "knowing man," and learning is the vehicle through which we come to know "who we are, where we came from, how the world works, and what matters in life," that is, "what it means to be human" (Pinker, 2018, p. 233).

I'm not talking here about the narrow conception of learning preservice teachers parrot back in their ed psych classes, that is, "learning is a change in behavior." Rats, dogs and porpoises can be trained to behave in certain ways given the right stimuli. That is part of the reason why joyful learning is hard to find in many classrooms. The education establishment has long been obsessed with accountability (Hatch, 2002), which often means applying principles developed with lab animals to the education of human beings. What I am talking about is using the human brain to process information in ways that no other being can. I am talking about tapping our capacities to think about our own thinking and get better at it. I am talking about a conception of learning that elevates it to the status of being necessary for us to fully experience our humanity. I am talking about ecstatic moments when we get lost within the experience of learning something valuable to our lives.

I did not go off and search the literature to find all I could about learning. My approach to teaching the kids in my Jacksonville class what learning is was to identify a particular skill or concept that each child needed to learn and then design a task that required the application of that skill or concept. I would then sit down with that child, and we would work on the task together until the child was able to do it alone. When the child was able to complete the task independently, we named what was happening and we celebrated together: "Look at what you learned! Look at how well your brain worked to figure this out! Look at how cool it feels to learn something important! Look at what a great learner you are!"

I experienced a terrific teacher preparation program at the University of Utah, but I had never read or even heard of Lev Vygotsky at that point in my life. But as I will discuss in Chapter 13 and other chapters, what I was doing in Jacksonville had a lot in common with the powerful lessons I learned later from reading Vygotsky (1962, 1978) in graduate school. I was, in effect, identifying tasks that kids could do with assistance but not alone and providing the support they needed until they could do the task independently—sounds a lot like scaffolding children's efforts within their zones of proximal development (Berk & Winsler, 1995; Stetsenko, 2016; Winsler, 2003).

In the process of trying to help my students discover what learning is and how to do it, I elevated my own love for learning—something that was and is a vital part of my life. Until this special teaching opportunity, my notions of learning stayed in the background—never fully exposed, examined, or expressed. Working in this special program helped me come to see the act of learning as one of the most important elements of my own life. In a pure expression of accidental good fortune, it turned out later that as a professor of education, I could make a living as a professional learner. The point is, I was not pretending to celebrate with the kids when they learned what learning is; my love of learning meant I was ecstatic right with them. What an amazing gift to share with young human beings: the gift of knowing what learning is, that it is a wonderful human experience, and that they can do it successfully.

Teachers who love their work always describe moments when "the light goes on in children's eyes"—the moments when the students understand something that has eluded them in the past. When these moments are real, kids are not just experiencing their success at learning some discrete skill, they are celebrating a realization that they are capable learners— something that is hard to come by unless teachers take the time to intentionally teach students the inherent value of learning and how to get better at it.

As teachers, we need to take every advantage of these special moments and bring to life the bigger point about the joy that should be part and parcel of the learning process. I'm not talking about the transitory fun I critiqued in Chapter 4; I'm trying to articulate the soul-stirring joy associated with learning as a human activity. Too much of what happens in too many classrooms is not joyful at all because it is too far removed from the kind of learning I am talking about here. In these classrooms, students are exposed to disconnected pieces of the standardized curriculum in preparation for some kind of high-stakes assessment. The high achievers are often bored, the average achievers put up with the routine as best they can, and the low achievers are mostly lost. This is not the fault of individual teachers; the system is set up to maximize accountability in the form of test score improvement.

The main point of this book is that individual teachers can and must bring more humanity back to the classroom. This chapter is about making sure that students have teachers who know how to satisfy the standardized expectations of the system at the same time they give the children with whom they work the gift of learning what learning is and how to revel in it.

In the special situation in Jacksonville and in my later elementary teaching, I made *learning* the centerpiece of what we were doing all the time, every day. We identified ourselves a "learning team," and we had a motto something like: "Learn a little every day." That is why the students were there and that is why I was there. We knew that standardized tests were going to happen, but no one ever said, "This is going to be on the Florida Standards Assessments." The learning itself was what counted. The learning process was what was emphasized. And, the inherent joy of learning was what was celebrated.

Even when new teachers do not feel like they have the autonomy I had in Jacksonville, I see plenty of space for teaching kids the joy of learning for its own sake. I have volunteered in urban schools where canned programs were closely monitored by "outside consultants" who routinely observed in classrooms to ensure that curricula purchased by the school system were implemented exactly as intended. Often assigned to work with students who were considered "bubble kids" (i.e., those the system identified as most likely to make progress enough to improve the school's value added test scores), I was often able to help them see themselves as capable learners who knew what genuine learning was all about. These kids mastered important skills and concepts and may have done better on the state mandated exams; but my aim was to change their perspective on learning and themselves as learners. I recall one powerful moment when one struggling child left my table, went directly to the teacher and proudly proclaimed, "Mrs. Jones, I can learn!"

Carol Dweck (1999, 2006) has done extensive research contrasting what she calls *performance* goals and *learning* goals. It is clear from her work that students internalize the values that the school engenders based on what they are expected to do and how they are evaluated. When performance goals are in place, successful students learn to play the school game and do just enough to pass the next test and move to the next grade level. They perform the tasks of school to get by, but see no meaningful connections to themselves or the world in which they live. Those who are not successful at playing the performance game either withdraw and disappear into the woodwork or rebel and do all they can to disrupt what they see as a meaningless system. In classrooms in which learning goals are emphasized, students internalize the value of learning for its own sake, live out the inherent virtue of effort and learning from one's mistakes, and celebrate the personal satisfaction that comes from persisting at important tasks.

Performance goals dominate what is happening in many schools today, especially those that serve students from low socioeconomic status and minority backgrounds. Operating schools based on performance-based assumptions limits young people's chances to experience learning as an exciting and fulfilling human activity. This means many students, including those who might benefit the most, are losing out. Systems are unlikely to change, but teachers can include much more emphasis on learning at the same time they do all they can to meet the expectations of an accountability regime based on standards-based performance goals.

Teaching students how to learn and showing them how to value themselves as learners does not involve special materials or computer programs—it is all about special kinds of interactions between someone who has acquired some important cultural knowledge and someone who needs to learn that knowledge (Rogoff, 2008; Stetsenko, 2016; Vygotsky, 1978). The interactions need to be focused on some concrete learning task that requires the application of the cultural knowledge in question. For example, skilled readers need to be able to make predictions based on information in the texts they are reading. Students need to use their brains to examine what the text says and then make a mental leap (an inference) to figure out what might logically follow. Further, students need to be able to utilize the text to justify the inferential predictions they make.

A task that gets directly at the cognitive processing needed to make predictions from text is easy to imagine. Teachers supply text that includes detail sufficient so that predictions can be made and justified. The student and teacher read the text together and then the teacher says they need to figure out what might happen next. The teacher then thinks out loud as he or she goes through the logic involved in figuring out what the text says that would provide a warrant for predicting what might happen next. As will be explained in detail in Chapter 13, the student will participate by providing as much input as possible and the teacher will release control of the learning situation gradually as the student begins to grasp the thinking involved.

The big idea is that the student and teacher are mutually engaged in the task, understanding that what the student can do with support (i.e., scaffolding) today, he or she will be able to do independently tomorrow (Berk & Winsler, 1995; Winsler, 2003). As the student increases his or her capacity to think inferentially and shows how to justify his or her predictions, the teacher withdraws and points out how well the student is using his or her brain and how great it is that he or she is learning this important skill. It is about the satisfaction of learning to predict from text; but it is also about intentionally learning the processes of learning and celebrating the joy of successfully utilizing those processes alongside someone who cares about you and cares about learning (Bransford et al., 1999; Hatch, 2005; Turner, 2011).

Again, what I was learning about learning early in my teaching career was reinforced in later studies of exactly what processes people, including children, utilize to become effective learners. For example, flying in the face to what has been assumed to be their limited cognitive capacities, brain researchers and cognitive scientists have discovered that even young children are fully capable of monitoring their own learning and intentionally getting better at it (Bransford et al., 1999; Hatch, 2020). But students do not acquire the skills needed for intentional learning by magic. They have to learn how to learn based on the support and scaffolding of competent adults. So, our students (even our youngest students) can learn to utilize sophisticated metacognitive lenses that allow them to see themselves as capable learners. Experiencing scaffolded, intentional instructional approaches like those in the example, they can learn what learning is and how to get better at it.

What a great opportunity we have as teachers! And what a massive responsibility! I tried to teach my students, my sons, and my grandkids that *you do not have to be perfect to be good*. From the doctoral candidate who cannot make himself write a dissertations because he is frozen with the fear that it will not be good enough to my fourth-grade granddaughter who is so used to excelling at everything she does that she sometimes shuts down when something does not come easy, the message is the same: What counts is not being perfect, but doing your best. His best will earn the advanced grad student his PhD and her best will show Breann that she can accomplish new things, even when they are tough.

In the classroom, what counts is doing your best to live out what you believe is right. As a new or preservice teacher, maybe you do not share my over-the-top love for learning; maybe you think the current accountability system will not allow you to create a classroom ethos where genuine human learning is the reason for everyone to be there; or maybe you think what I am talking about does not make sense in the complex contexts of the digital, global, postmodern world of the 21st century. But if any part of what I am saying about the inherent value of learning rings true for you—if you believe it is *right* to put more emphasis on engaging students in meaningful tasks and scaffolding their learning about learning and themselves as learners—then (even if you are not going to be perfect) you have to do your best to live out that belief.

No matter where you are in your teaching journey, it is not too early or too late to reassess your own relationship to learning. You may not be processing the same kinds of information I am. You may not even be processing information using the same modalities I usually use. But, you must have experienced moments when you got involved in what you were reading/seeing/hearing/doing to the point that you felt the joy of getting lost in the experience.

Decades ago, Abraham Maslow (1968) described peak experiences, during which individuals become so engaged in a fulfilling activity that they experience their full humanity and lose track of everything except the moment itself. Maslow believed that children were capable of having peak experiences (Hoffman, 2011), and others have shown that certain educational activities can foster peak experiences in students (Yair, 2008). As a teacher, I believe you have the opportunity to create those kinds of ecstatic experiences for your students and yourself. Whatever platforms and texts you are utilizing, you can put more attention on growing the act of learning and nurturing its place in your classroom.

As a new or future teacher, I invite you to stop and think carefully about why we have schools and what our place should be in the schools in which we work. Without a clear purpose, schooling and teaching can become uninteresting, inert, and ineffective. Teaching is torture for teachers and their students when educators just put in their time and collect their pay. If learning goals could replace the current emphasis on performance goals in school, then the purposes of school could be redefined in ways that make humanity and meaning important in the classroom.

I do not think it will be easy for teachers to alter the performance-driven purposes of schooling; but I do think teachers can bring more meaning to our classrooms than we currently do. As a teacher, you will have spaces to emphasize learning over performance. You will have opportunities to scaffold students' efforts to learn what learning is and to experience themselves as competent learners. You will have the chance to show kids that learning is a vital part of what makes them human and that there is genuine, exhilarating, freeing joy in learning and being a learner. You do not have to be perfect at it to be good. You do not have to make every moment an ecstatic experience to make a difference. You do have to be true to yourself and honor your commitment to touching the lives of children in important positive ways. What counts is doing your level best in the classroom and in life to enact what you know in your heart of hearts is the right thing to do.

REFERENCES

Berk, L. E., & Winsler, A. (1995). *Scaffolding children's learning: Vygotsky and early childhood education*. National Association for the Education of Young Children.

Bransford, J. D., Brown, A. L., & Cocking, R. R. (1999). *How people learn: Brain, mind, experience, and school*. National Academy Press.

Choi, C. Q. (2016, March 25). *Top 10 things that make humans special*. Live Science. https://www.livescience.com/15689-evolution-human-special-species.html

Dweck, C. S. (1999). *Self-theories: Their role in motivation, personality and development*. Psychology Press.

Dweck, C. S. (2006). *Mindset: The new psychology of success*. Random House.

Hatch, J. A. (2002). Accountability shovedown: Resisting the standards movement in early childhood education. *Phi Delta Kappan, 83*, 457–462.

Hatch, J. A. (2005). *Teaching in the new kindergarten*. Thomson Delmar Learning.

Hatch, J. A. (2020). From theory to curriculum: Developmental theory and its relationship to curriculum and instruction in early childhood education. In J. J. Mueller & N. File (Eds.), *Curriculum in early childhood education: Re-examined, rediscovered, renewed* (pp. 51–63). Routledge.

Hoffman, E. (2011, September 4). The peak experience. *Psychology Today*. https://www.psychologytoday.com/us/blog/the-peak-experience/201109/what-was-maslows-view-peak-experiences

Maslow, A. H. (1968). *Toward a psychology of being*. Van Nostrand Reinhold.

Pinker, S. (2018). *Enlightenment now: The case for reason, science, humanism, and progress*. Viking.

Rogoff, B. (2008). Observing sociocultural activity on three planes: Participatory appropriation, guided participation, and apprenticeship. In P. Murphy, K. Hall, K., & Soler, J. (Eds.), *Pedagogy and practice: Culture and identities* (pp. 58–74). SAGE.

Stetsenko, A. (2016). *The transformative mind: Expanding Vygotsky's approach to development and education.* Cambridge University Press.

Swadener, B. B., & Lubeck, S. (1995). *Children and families "at promise:" Deconstructing the discourse of risk.* State University of New York Press.

Turner, S. L. (2011). Student-centered instruction: Integrating the learning sciences to support elementary and middle school learners. *Preventing School Failure, 55*(3), 123–131.

Vygotsky, L. S. (1962). *Thought and language.* MIT Press.

Vygotsky, L. S. (1978). *Mind and society: The development of higher mental processes.* Harvard University Press.

Winsler, A. (Ed.) (2003). Vygotskian perspectives in early childhood education: Translating ideas into classroom practice [Special issue]. *Early Education and Development, 14*(3).

Yair, G. (2008). Key educational experiences and self-discovery in higher education. *Teaching and Teacher Education. 24,* 92–103.

CHAPTER 7

LOVING STUDENTS IS NOT ENOUGH; TEACHERS NEED TO BE WARM DEMANDERS

All parents want teachers who care about their children; but no one wants teachers whose love for children gets in the way of students being successful in school or life. Many parents are worried that some "caring" teachers are short-changing their children. They want to say to these teachers: "I know you mean well, but do not love my child so much that you expect anything less than the very best from him!" The concept of "warm demanders" from the literature on working with students from diverse backgrounds is used in this chapter to show how teachers can express their caring most vitally by settling for nothing less than each student's personal best in the classroom. Examples and counter examples are provided to show what warm demanding looks like in a variety of classrooms.

Virtually all of my classroom teaching experience was in urban schools populated by kids from underserved backgrounds, and the majority of my university work has been focused on schooling in urban-multicultural settings. I have learned a lot from my colleagues and students at both the school and university levels. One of the concepts that is most compelling to me in my work in preparing urban teachers is the notion of teachers as "warm demanders." I feel a little uneasy about adopting the language and logic of this concept and applying it to classroom teaching in any setting.

Teaching as a Human Activity: Ways to Make Classrooms Joyful and Effective
pp. 55–62

This book is designed to be of support and inspiration for all teachers, not just those who work in diverse urban schools. I am hoping I can frame what I see as the critical elements of the warm demander concept so that I give due credit to those who pioneered these ideas, while providing a valuable instructional stance for teachers in a variety of settings.

The warm demander construct has its roots in the literature on culturally responsive teaching (Gay, 2010; Irvine & Fraser, 1998; Ladson-Billings, 1994; Ware, 2006). The aim of culturally responsive teaching is to empower African American students "intellectually, socially, emotionally, and politically by using cultural referents to impart knowledge, skills, and attitudes" (Ladson-Billings, 1994, p. 382). Warm demanding is a stance that teachers take as part of their culturally responsive pedagogical approach. Teachers who are warm demanders adopt a no-nonsense, tough-minded, authoritative teaching stance with their students, insisting that they "not only *can* learn but *must* learn" (Irvin & Foster, 1998, p. 56). These teachers' tough-minded approach is based in their commitment to do all they can to ensure the success of their students in the classroom and in life. They are perceived as "warm" by their students, communities, and families not because they appear to be caring and nice; they are admired because they accept no excuses, have high standards, and demand that students do their best (Wilson & Corbett, 2001). Warm demanders have high expectations that they refuse to compromise, but they realize that students need support in order to meet those expectations—so these teachers are willing to do whatever it takes to ensure student success (Ware, 2006).

Two terrific colleagues of mine from my doctoral study days at the University of Florida have done some important work applying the warm demander construct to the preparation of teachers, most of whom are not African American. Elizabeth Bondy and Dorene Ross have provided a useful framework for thinking about how warm demanding might look in a variety of settings (Bondy & Ross, 2008). Based on their interpretations and experiences, these two scholars and some of their current colleagues have researched the impact of White teachers applying warm demander pedagogical practices in classrooms with majority African American students (Bondy et. al., 2012). I will rely on my friends' work to put a frame around my discussion of ways teachers in any setting can apply understandings about warm demanders to improve relations, behavior, and performance in their classrooms.

To organize my discussion, I want to talk about the "warm" part, then the "demander" part of this approach. Within each part, I will pick out elements of the warm demander concept and give examples and non-examples of what that element might look like in practice. Again, the elements below are based on the efforts of the teachers and scholars (many of whom are cited above) who have developed the warm demander construct as part of the literature on culturally responsive teaching.

WHAT DOES A WARM TEACHER LOOK LIKE AND NOT LOOK LIKE?

A warm teacher has a personal connection with each of her students. That means that she makes it clear that she has a genuine interest in them as human beings. That means she talks directly to them, asks real questions about their lives, takes time to actively listen to what they have to say, holds her body and her eyes in an attitude that shows she is engaged and paying attention, and makes meaningful responses to their comments. Warm teachers send the message that they care about what their students think and have to say. As will become clear below, these signs of warmth do not mean that teachers want to erase their role as the adult in the room. The opposite is true: They want to be the caring adult in the room who is willing to take responsibility for doing whatever is necessary to ensure the success of every student. Warm teachers realize that relationships take time to develop. They know that all relationships are two-way streets and never perfect—so they are willing to let them develop and are ready to work on repairing them when relationships hit rough spots.

Teachers will not be perceived as warm when they are distant or aloof, positioning themselves as oblivious to the individual personalities and experiences of their students. Such teachers hide behind their role and send the message that who the students are as people has no bearing on life in school. These teachers avoid having meaningful interactions with their students. They do not have occasion to actually listen to students or to respond in ways that acknowledge the humanity of the young people in their classrooms. They use their eyes, body, and tone of voice to signal that human interaction is not a part of what is important in school. They may have high expectations for kids, but those kids will often shut down or resist because school assignments will seem like arbitrary orders from a taskmaster, instead of being perceived as a challenge they share with someone who knows them and cares about their success.

A warm teacher learns about her students' cultural backgrounds. This is a defining element of culturally responsive teaching and critical to being a warm demander. Warm teachers who come from cultures that differ from those of their students are aware of the potential biases they might bring to interactions in the classroom and community, and they work to mitigate those biases by being open to learning all they can about the values, beliefs, and practices of the cultures around them. Warm teachers do not see differences in cultural backgrounds as obstacles to learning, but as sources of strength to be valued and built upon. These teachers spend time in the communities they serve, attending meetings, visiting churches, going to sporting events, joining celebrations. They talk with students about the music they love, the places they hang out, the food they enjoy. They meet with parents wherever those parents can or want to meet—in homes, in community centers, in local restaurants, in school (Delpit, 1995). They send the message to their students, families, and communities that, "I value individuals as cultural beings and I want to learn all I can so I can be the best teacher I can be."

Teachers will not be perceived as warm if they pretend to be "color-blind" or act as if their job is to implement a set of stock methods and approaches so that everyone will come out the same at the end of the education process. Surely we have figured out by now that statements like, "I do not see color; I only see children" are self-deluding at best, and downright hurtful at worst. Teachers will not be seen as warm when they work from the assumption that either culture does not matter in school or that it is their job to pass along the majority White culture embedded in the standard curriculum and assessment system currently in place. These teachers will focus on marching through the scopes and sequences of their subject matter in an attempt to improve scores on the inevitable high-stakes tests. Connecting to their students' backgrounds will be seen as a distraction, and learning about the cultural experiences surrounding school will not even come to mind. They will show up at school, do their job, then head back to their home neighborhoods.

A warm teacher believes in her students and lets them know that she does. There are two tightly linked parts here: (1) the teacher has to know in the core of her being that every student can be successful; and (2) she has to be able to communicate that confidence to her students. Without 1, there can be no 2. Without 2, 1 is a moot point. So, I did not say the teacher had to believe each child was going to be earning a full-ride scholarship to Harvard. It is the job of a professional educator to take each child where he is and move him to the next level. Each kid needs to know that he can learn—that he can do what is necessary to be successful in accomplishing school tasks. Students come to know that they are capable of learning because teachers tell them they are *and* because teachers show them that they are (see sections below and Chapters 2 and 13 in this book).

Teachers will not be perceived as warm if they whisper to kids they are smart but set up countless opportunities to fail—opportunities that shout out their status as poor learners. Students know when their teachers think they are incapable of learning, even when the signals are subtle. Young people will not be fooled by empty praise or conned into thinking they are brilliant for accomplishing tasks that are dumbed down. Unhappily, some teachers are not even subtle in signaling their feelings about student capacities. These teachers use sarcasm, overgeneralization, blaming, and even overtly racist statements to put students down. You are not a warm teacher if you say things like: "I guess you were too busy talking to your friends to finish the assignment;" "You never pay attention to anything I say to you;" "It is your own fault for not following directions;" "You people will never be successful until you stop acting like fools."

Children and young people know when they are being patronized, devalued or insulted. They know when their teachers are just putting in time in order to draw a paycheck. They know when teachers cannot or will not see them as individuals and cultural beings. They also know when their teachers are doing their best to meet the criteria for being warm teachers as described here. But being warm is necessary but not sufficient for facilitating student success. Warm teachers need to be demanding too.

WHAT DOES A DEMANDING TEACHER LOOK LIKE AND NOT LOOK LIKE?

A demanding teacher is clear and consistent about her expectations in the classroom. She is authoritative. She says what she means and means what she says. Instead of asking students if they want to put their things away and move on to the next activity, she tells them exactly what they are to do and when. She does not negotiate the consequences of actions that have been prescribed as inappropriate; she gives opportunities for students to do the right thing when rules are broken but calmly applies consequences without expressing anger, bitterness, or any sense of retribution. She never makes idle threats, and always follows through when setting the high standards for behavior in the classroom.

A teacher will not be perceived as demanding when she gets caught up in debating with students about what they did or what should happen because of their misbehavior. She will not be respected as demanding if she adopts a strict authoritarian stance, in which she expects to use the power of her role to dominate her students. As we will see in Chapter 11, teachers never win power struggles with their students. Neither will it work if she comes off as a laissez-faire teacher who acts more like a friend than the adult in charge, always offering one more chance and letting things get out of hand because her kids see the limits as always fluid and the consequences as always negotiable. A teacher will not be treated as demanding when her students learn that she has buttons to be pushed based on her emotional reactions in the classroom. By responding in ways that display distress, anger, or frustration, teachers reveal vulnerabilities that students catalog and store for use later on.

A demanding teacher adopts a no excuses philosophy that permeates everything that happens in the classroom (Wilson & Corbett, 2001). There is no bemoaning that, "Oh, these kids have it so rough at home we are lucky they even come to school" or rationalizing that, "Education is just not valued in the community" or grousing that, "I feel lucky just getting through the day without a major disruption." Demanding teachers insist that every student does his best every day. They insist that students learn because they must learn in order to be successful in school and in life (Ware, 2006). They insist that students show respect for their teachers and their classmates. Students accept this insistent stance because, by being demanding, teachers demonstrate that the students are "important enough to be pushed, disciplined, taught, and respected" (Wilson & Corbett, 2001, p. 88).

A teacher will not be perceived as demanding when she feels sorry for students, expects them to perform poorly, or creates or accepts excuses for less than full-on best effort. It is an unfortunate irony that some of the folks who want to work in high need areas (e.g., social work, special education, or schools serving kids from under-served families) are there because they feel sorry to the populations they work with. They see big needs and are sometimes on a mission to "save" their clients or students. Demanding teachers do not see students or families that need saving— they see capable people who will succeed given the right opportunity and support. Likewise, teachers will not be perceived as demanding if they expect less than exceptional performance from their students. Telling or showing students that the expectations are lower for them because of their circumstances or their capabilities is a self-fulfilling prophecy waiting to come true. Further, no excuses means no excuses; and teachers will not be perceived as demanding when they find ways to explain away their lack of success or bend to their students' alibis for not putting forth their best efforts.

A demanding teacher provides the supports students need to be successful and never gives up when things do not go perfectly. Just hoping or wishing or expecting learning to happen will never work by itself. Making sure students learn is the basic job of a demanding teacher. That means meeting the students where they are, charting a challenging but achievable pathway to success, then providing the instruction and support necessary to move them along that pathway. It means being willing and able to present material in a variety of ways. It means breaking complex learning down into manageable segments and showing students how those segments fit into the larger concepts, skills, and dispositions being taught. It means scaffolding learning so that students are presented with tasks that they cannot do independently but can do with the intentional support of the teacher (see Chapter 13). It means that teachers never give up on their students and always look for ways to make material more accessible. It means teachers never blame students for not getting it and always take responsibility for making sure everyone has the opportunity succeed.

A teacher will not be perceived as demanding when she presents material in one way and expects the students to get it or not, moving on to the next bit of curriculum using the same method. This approach only works when the teacher's methods are well-suited for every student and the content is mastered at each step of the process. It falls apart when students learn in different ways than are being used or when students do not have the prerequisite understandings to process the new information. Unfortunately, some of the elements that keep many kids from being successful are built into canned programs and pacing guides provided by textbook companies and many school systems. Teachers are told what to teach, how to teach, and when to teach certain content. If students get behind under these regimens, they are bound to get farther behind. Demanding teachers are there to teach children and young people, not to march through the curriculum or implement perpetual test prep. They take responsibility for finding ways to work around programs and policies that limit their students' chances for success. Teachers who do not qualify as demanding throw up their hands and say, "My kids do not understand _____, but we have to stay on schedule and move on to _____." And they sometimes deflect responsibility and say things like: "These kids just cannot learn;" "These kids just do not try;" or "These kids are so far behind that they are destined to fail."

In sum, warm demanding teachers create a classroom culture in which success is taken to be the non-negotiable norm. They show their warmth by demanding that students put forth their best effort, show respect for their teachers and peers, and never give up. They teach in ways that maximize everyone's chances for success. They support positive behavior, accept problems as normal, and work with students to find solutions (Bondy & Ross, 2008). A student in Cushman's (2003) interview study of high school students summarized how teachers can create such a classroom culture: "Remind us often you expect our best, encourage our efforts even if we are having trouble, give helpful feedback … don't compare us to other students, and stick with us" (pp. 64–67).

I believe that teachers in all settings can learn something from those who have developed and practiced the warm demander approach. An essential part of the premise here is knowing the communities in which you are teaching. Learning all you can about the cultures, backgrounds, and experiences of your students is essential in any setting. Based on those understandings, the application of the warm demander construct can be an invaluable tool for making sure every child has every opportunity to be successful in school. At the very least, it thoroughly dispels the myth that being nice means expecting less from any child. It provides a powerful reminder that loving children means the opposite of feeling sorry for them—it means holding them in enough esteem to expect nothing but their best.

REFERENCES

Bondy, E., & Ross, D. D. (2008). The teacher as warm demander. *Educational Leadership, 66*(1), 54–58.

Bondy, E., Ross, D. D., Hambacher, E., & Acosta, M. (2012). Becoming warm demanders: Perspectives and practices of first year teachers. *Urban Education, 48*(3), 420–450.

Cushman, K. (2003). *Fires in the bathroom: Advice for teachers from high school students.* The New Press.

Delpit, L. (1995). *Other people's children: Cultural conflict in the classroom.* The New Press.

Gay, G. (2010). *Culturally responsive teaching: Theory, research, and practice.* Teachers College Press.

Irvine, J. J., & Fraser, J. (1998). Warm demanders: Do national certification standards leave room for the culturally responsive pedagogy of African American teachers? *Education Week, 17*(35), 56.

Ladson-Billings, G. (1994). *The dreamkeepers: Successful teachers of African American children.* Jossey-Bass.

Ware, F. (2006). Warm demander pedagogy: Culturally responsive teaching that supports a culture of achievement for African American students. *Urban Education, 41*, 427–456.

Wilson, B. L., & Corbett, H. D. (2001). *Listening to urban kids: School reform and the teachers they want.* State University of New York Press.

CHAPTER 8

TEACHING FOCUSED ON HUMAN PROCESSES COULD MAKE SCHOOL MORE MEANINGFUL TO STUDENTS AND TEACHERS

I am old, and this chapter is based on an old idea. The original thinkers behind this idea were an inspiration to me when I was doing my advanced doctoral studies. My PhD is in curriculum and instruction, and at the University of Florida we could not leave the program without a heavy dose of *curriculum* (what is to be taught) and *instruction* (how to teach it). This is where I became intrigued with the work of curriculum pioneer Louise Berman. For me, her most important book was a rationale for challenging traditional ways of organizing school content around subject-matter areas and, instead, centering school curriculum around the processes that define our humanness. Berman's book was aptly titled, *New Priorities in the Curriculum* and was first published in 1968. I said I was old.

The basic premise that you could build curriculum around human processes never got a foothold in education, although others have tried to build on Berman's ideas over the years (e.g., Cole, 1972; Hatch, 1984). I know that one short chapter in one little book is not going to change the face of curriculum organization in U. S. schools, but I am hoping that I can convince you that you can make your classroom a much

Teaching as a Human Activity: Ways to Make Classrooms Joyful and Effective
pp. 63–73
Copyright © 2021 by Information Age Publishing
All rights of reproduction in any form reserved.

more engaging, meaningful, and human place by taking the ideas outlined here seriously. The point will not be to replace the standard curriculum with a totally new set of concepts, skills, and dispositions. The argument here is for you as a teacher to consider reorganizing at least part of what is to be covered in your classroom and present material in a form that directly relates to a set of human processes.

Berman (1968) described eight process skills "necessary to get at the essence of human living and understanding: perceiving, communicating, loving, knowing, decision making, patterning, creating, and valuing" (p. 11). I will not try to illuminate all of Berman's process skills, but the ones I have selected represent distinctly human processes that could be used as a framework for presenting school content in a different and more meaningful way. The processes I have chosen to focus on are perceiving, communicating, and patterning. Again, although I think it would be a wonderful change to rethink the ways the whole curriculum is organized, my goals here are much more modest. I want to suggest that teachers step back from the curriculum content that it is their job to teach and consider presenting at least some of that content organized into units, themes, projects, or some other creative form that focuses on human processes. After I talk a bit more about why this approach is important, I will discuss the three selected process skills, describing ways teachers at various levels of schooling can apply these ideas across a variety of subject-matter areas.

Instead of dividing what needs to be learned into separate subjects that rarely cross paths and thinking of content as a set of unrelated, hierarchically arranged skills and concepts, wouldn't it be powerful to rethink the school curriculum so that it is overtly linked to the humanness of each student and teacher? When you are applying a human processes approach, content from the different disciplines is not taught as isolated, disconnected knowledge to be mastered in order to pass a test; but knowledge, skills, and dispositions are learned within a curriculum framework focused on the very processes that make each of us distinct from other living things. The emphasis switches from mastering discrete bits of knowledge to maximizing the development of human potential. Such a shift gives direct, readily apparent meaning to the activities of school. I believe an emphasis on human processes can be utilized in any classroom to enhance students' engagement, bring more meaning to what goes on day to day, improve everyone's chances of learning content that fits somewhere in their lives, and boost both students' and teachers' excitement about the learning process. Examples across grade levels and subject areas follow.

PERCEIVING (A PRIMARY GRADE THEME STUDY)

Berman (1968) calls perceiving "the basis and stimulus for other human functions" (p. 40). I agree. When I taught kindergarten and primary-age students what makes humans different from other living things, I emphasized the amazing complexity of our brains. None of the processes we are talking about in this chapter are possible in other animals because they do not have the same intellectual capabilities as human beings. This is true for perceiving. Other living things react to their environments—plants turn toward sunlight and scavengers follow odors to locate carrion. Other living things experience sensations, but there is no cognitive attempt to grasp their meaning. They react to stimuli, but they are not utilizing the highly sophisticated brain power humans use to make sense of all of the information that surrounds them. Perception is important because it is the avenue carrying all the raw material that makes human brainwork possible.

When you think about it, we do not do very much, if anything, to help students get better at perceiving the world around them. It is taken for granted that when we present material, young people are practicing their capacities of perception—but why leave it to chance? Savvy art teachers and science instructors teach students to carefully examine the world around them, but as a rule, teaching children what perceiving is and how they can get better at it does not happen much in school. This may be a serious oversight, given that perceiving is the conduit through which new information enters the brain.

By way of example, I describe how a theme study of perceiving might be planned and presented in a primary classroom. As with the examples in the next sections, these are just possibilities. They are meant to get your thinking started by illuminating ways to engage students in the study of a human process—ways that utilize important content from a variety of disciplines, while focusing attention on maximize potential through developing a particular dimension of humanness.

A study of perceiving could start with an exploration of how information gets from the outside world into our brains. In theme studies, you want to organize as many activities as you can around your theme. In the kindergarten and primary grades, these often take form as studies of topics like ocean life, families, poetry, or the works of a favorite children's author. So teachers develop activities (often for a week's time) that incorporate math, language arts, science, social studies, art, and physical education into the chosen theme. The same general approach could be taken in developing a thematic study of perceiving.

Thematic studies are often introduced with some kind of grabber that orients students to the theme and gets them thinking about what they are about to learn and why. An opening grabber for the perceiving theme could be as simple as having the class close their eyes and just listen for 30 seconds, then talking about what they heard. Depending on their age, the students could be led to think about how they recognized what they heard or how much sound surrounds them that they pay no attention to, except when strategically listening. This grabber can set the stage for presenting a series of activities that involve taking in information from the environment via the senses. The point here will not be to teach the body part associated with each of the five senses (the standard fare of the primary science curriculum) but to explore how input from the environment enters the brain through the senses and what the human brain does with that data that other living things cannot do.

Some possible theme-based lessons that focus on this human process and integrate understandings from the usual primary curriculum include:

- Activities that parallel the stop and listen introductory lesson could be designed for each sensory pathway. For example, students could be given a cloth bag holding an object that they have to identify based only on reaching into the bag to feel it. Or, vials with strong smelling scents could be spread around the room and students rotated among the vials recording what they think the smells are in observation journals. Or, students could be blindfolded and asked to identify the ethnic origins of different foods just by tasting them. Or, students could be asked to write down as many objects as are within their field of vision that contain the geometric shapes they have been studying. With all activities of this type, teachers need to be explicit about how only humans use their senses and brains to understand their surroundings and that they can improve their understanding by being better perceivers and thinkers.

- Students could take a walking field trip to collect leaves. Returning to the classroom, they could inspect them with magnifying glasses, sort them into like sets based on their characteristics, use print or electronic sources to identify the trees from which the leaves came, then make detailed drawings that show the elements that make the leaf types unique. A discussion of the importance of careful observation and attention to detail should follow, along with reminders of how the brain uses perceptual data to organize our understandings of the world.

- Students could be divided into small groups and each group given an object that they are to describe to the rest of the group by writing in adjectives based on the following prompts: It looks _____; It sounds _____; It feels _____; It tastes _____; It smells _____. Each group shares its adjectives and the rest of the class tries to guess their object. This activity is concluded with a discussion of how some senses were more important than others in describing the object, how the brain decides what objects are being described, and how the brain identifies new objects the first time they are encountered.

- Young students can apply what they have learned about perceiving by completing activities that ask them to identify which sense or senses would be needed to form conclusions based on information from the environment. For example, what sense or senses would be used to figure out:

  o a jet was flying overhead;
  o the burner on the stove was turned on;
  o the peach was not ripe;
  o the milk had gone sour; or
  o lunch was ready?

With this and all the sample activities, the key is to help students see the links to the human process being studied. Just doing the activities may have some merit, but the power of this approach will be greatly diminished unless kids know how important these processes are and how they can get better at utilizing them. As Berman (1968) summarizes, "Young people will grow up to handle their lives more effectively if they have learned the wonder of perception, for perceiving is indeed the basis and stimulus for other human functions" (p. 40).

COMMUNICATING (LANGUAGE ARTS ACTIVITIES FOR INTERMEDIATE AND MIDDLE GRADES)

For Berman (1968), communicating is the sharing of personal meaning. While other animals produce noises to sound alarms or attract mates, using abstract signs and symbols to share meaning is reserved for human beings. Berman acknowledges that developing the traditional skills associated with reading, writing, speaking and listening is important, but only so far as these skills make young people better able to share meanings with others.

This take on communicating as a human process puts the emphasis on learning to get better at participating in interactive events through which thoughts, feelings, and intentions are exchanged between self and others. The example explored here is designed to help children and young people see that the ability to share meaning with others through verbal communication is vital to their success and happiness as developing human beings. Speaking and listening are elevated to the status of essential elements of human behavior, so improving the ability to verbally communicate generates its own meaningfulness, motivation, and momentum.

I think of communication as having two modes: expressive and receptive. Speaking and writing are expressive modes, while listening and reading fit on the receptive side. In order to get better at sharing meanings with others, students need opportunities to understand and practice elements from both modes. Because of space, only examples of activities for improving speaking and listening will be presented here. Sample activities focused on improving verbal communication are outlined below. The pattern will be to present lessons meant to introduce new content or enrich student understandings, followed by activities designed to allow them to practice applying those understandings.

Speaking is verbal expressive language. Upper elementary and middle school students can learn that communicating (i.e., sharing meaning) depends on their ability to put their thoughts into words that can be understood by those with whom they interact. They can come to realize that unless their verbal messages are interpreted in the ways they were intended, communication has broken down. Teachers can build their students' understanding of the reciprocal relationship between speaker and listener by presenting descriptions of how these systems work and providing examples and nonexamples of effective verbal communication.

An example of a way to practice speaking clearly and with a purpose to a particular audience would be to assign students to pairs and have them alternate the roles of speaker and listener, while their conversations are being audio or video recorded. One student could be assigned to explain his or her favorite leisure activity to someone who has never seen nor heard of that activity. Or, one student could retell a familiar fairy tale as if speaking to a younger child who has never heard it. Or, one student could give directions for walking from one location to another as if talking to someone from outside the community. The recordings could then be played back (as many times as needed) so students could learn to analyze when their communications were clear and when they needed to make adjustments. New recordings could be made and compared to originals to assess improvements and tweak future attempts.

Listening is the receptive side of verbal communication. When sharing personal meaning is seen as the goal of communicating and speaking and listening are paired as reciprocal tools for generating shared understanding, it makes sense to help students get better at both. Within a human processes curriculum approach, children and young people need to understand that shared meaning is constructed in the give and take of verbal communication—that listeners have a responsibility to work with speakers to *make meaning* together. They can be taught what effective listening looks like and what it does not look like, and they can practice the skills that improve the chances of meaningful verbal exchange. Some examples of activities to improve listening skills are presented below. These parallel active listening strategies described in fields such as education, psychology, and business (e.g., Leonardo, 2020; Patterson et al., 2011) and complement the social skills example described in Chapter 3.

Practicing the kind of listening we are talking about here would mean giving kids opportunities to engage in conversations with others and monitoring how well they are making those conversations active attempts at achieving shared meaning. Again, using audio or (especially) video technologies to record and analyze conversations provides immediate feedback, and students can be paired up within the classroom as above. In addition, opportunities for conversations between your students and students from higher grade levels could be arranged. These could be set up as interviews in order to find out what upper elementary kids should know about life in middle school or what middle schoolers should expect in high school. Or, your students could be part of a class oral history project, with the assignment of interviewing someone from their family who can give a unique perspective on important events or milestones in the past. In preparation for either task, students would put together a list of questions to guide their interviews; but they also must be prepared to exercise listening skills that will bring richness and meaning sharing to the interview interactions. Some of the skills they need to learn and practice are listed below, along with statements or questions that demonstrate the enactment of the skill in conversation:

- Repeating what you heard in your own words (e.g., "It sounds like you...")
- Asking for elaboration ("Can you say more about _____?")
- Asking for examples ("Can you think of a specific example of _____?")
- Using your body to express interest and engagement (holding eye contact, leaning forward, nodding and smiling, keeping a relaxed posture)
- Waiting for your turn to speak (doing your best to try to understand what your partner is saying rather than interrupting or composing your response while she is speaking).

Using spoken and written language to communicate is a major factor in defining our humanness. Finding ways to get better at sharing meaning together is a worthy goal for any school curriculum, and as teachers, we can find ways to reframe the ways we organize instruction so that this goal is accomplished and our students enhance their communication skills and their human potential.

PATTERNING (A UNIT STUDY FOR HIGH SCHOOL)

Units are traditional ways of organizing curriculum. They usually have a linear design, building knowledge and skills within a particular subject matter area. Units in high school are often a series of lessons that build on each other and cover a number of related instructional objectives. Some examples across the secondary curriculum could include units on: polynomials; homeostasis; World War II; romanticism; or nutrition. The sample unit elements described here are based in biology and English, but units exploring how knowledge is patterned could be developed in any subject matter discipline that has an organized body of knowledge. As above, the activities of the unit address many objectives from the standard curriculum, but the emphasis is placed on studying patterning as a uniquely human process.

Rereading Berman's (1968) *New Priorities in the Curriculum* for the preparation of this chapter, I was a little troubled by what she seemed to be saying about patterning. I love the idea that humans organize knowledge systematically, and I have been teaching for years that young people can benefit greatly from understanding how those taxonomies of concepts, generalizations, and theories are organized, created, expanded, and sometimes discarded. For me, developing that understanding in students has been the essence of teaching patterning as a human process. Studying Berman now, I am not sure she would think my approach goes far enough. Her chapter has a clear emphasis on children learning "how to pattern or systematize" (p. 120). It is the *how* part that I have given short shrift to over the years. As I present examples of elements that could be included in a unit study of patterning, I will try to have it both ways.

A study of patterning is all about seeing relationships among different pieces of information. It is a careful examination of how what is known is categorized so that we can keep track of it, add to it, and change it when we figure out something is amiss. Categories of knowledge are formulated so they facilitate the storage and retrieval of vital information. Without taxonomies of knowledge and experience, every bit of new data that enters the brain via the senses would have to be processed as unique input and the brain would be immediately overwhelmed. Humans have the capacity to organize what they know in categories into which new information can comfortably be placed, or they can make new categories because the new information does not fit categories they already have.

Piaget famously called the categories *schema* and the processes described as *assimilation* and *accommodation* (Piaget & Cook, 1952).

Just as individuals have the capacity to discover the patterns in experience and construct categories for processing new information, so do scholars and other close observers have tools for organizing the broad expanse of knowledge that makes up what is known about the world. Subject matter disciplines have evolved that each lay claim to a body of knowledge that they count as their purview. The knowledge within each discipline has been categorized in ways that show relationships among individual parts and make possible the assimilation of new information or the accommodation of new categories.

A teacher of any high school subject could build a unit around the knowledge base most closely associated with her disciplinary base. For the sake of example, I will start by describing some possible activities for a unit on patterning in a general biology class. The unit could start with an overview of the necessity of organizing disciplinary knowledge for the reasons outlined above. Early on, students could be taught (or reminded) of how concepts can be hierarchically organized into subordinates, coordinates, and superordinates. Understanding these relationships is key to understanding how categories are formed, and activities could be designed to help students see how our knowledge of living things is organized into taxonomies based on these relationships. For example, students could be asked to identify subordinate concepts that would fit under the category of marsupials (e.g., kangaroos, wallabies, opossums, etc.); then identify coordinate concepts for marsupials (monotremes and placentals); then a superordinate category under which marsupials can be classified (mammals). With these basic understandings, students could be assigned to groups with the responsibility for generating biological taxonomies at any level of complexity of which they are capable.

In English, a unit that gives students the opportunity to generate their own patterns could be designed around an analysis of characters in graphic novels. If the emphasis is to be placed on helping young people learn how to create organizers (rather than apply them), then students need the opportunity to think inductively, putting together specific instances in order to construct generalizations. Therefore, teachers would not start with a "textbook" formula for thinking about character analysis (the usual, deductive way this is usually taught). Instead, teachers would give students opportunities to work individually and/or in groups to look at characters across novels, generating statements that describe elements that make the characters stand out in the story. Once statements are produced, students can work together or on their own to determine which statements can be grouped together, and the beginnings of an outline that organizes what the students are learning about graphic novel characters can be created. As new insights from new novels are processed, out-lines can be expanded or modified. Since the emphasis is on human *processes*, as with all the activities above, students need to know that it is the process of creating their own knowledge organization that is most important here. We want them to experience the different kind of brain-work needed to think inductively and to see how they are capable of the same kind of thinking used by those who organize the knowledge base in any field.

The goal of this chapter, section, and book is to get you thinking about ways to organize your teaching so that your students see more meaning in what they are studying. Focusing on human processes seems like a great way to move in that direction. I tried to give enough detail and examples to get you grounded in ways to emphasize the human processes of per-ceiving, communication, and patterning. I conclude with definitions of how Berman (1968) conceptualized the other human processes in her list.

- Loving: "Coresponding" (the ability to give and receive love) is seen as a vital and powerful human process that needs to be exam-ined and developed in school (p. 63).
- Knowing: Students need to study the nature of knowing and to see themselves as able to learn, create, and utilize knowledge.
- Decisionmaking: School ought to be a place where young people learn that decision making can be "a turning point between the past and the future," and they should be given tools to improve the quality of the decisions they make (p. 105).
- Creating: Students need opportunities to "reach for the unprece-dented" and to gain competence in the various components of the creative process (p. 138).
- Valuing: Students need to learn about and have opportunities to apply ethical thinking—they need to confront value questions (questions of "should" and "ought") (p. 174).

I hope these will stir your thinking and invite possibilities for reorganiz-ing at least a small part of the curriculum in ways that bring more human-ness to your classroom.

REFERENCES

Berman, L. M. (1968). *New priorities in the curriculum.* C. E. Merrill.
Cole, H. P. (1972). *Process education.* Educational Technology Publications.
Hatch, J. A. (1984). Technology and the devaluation of human processes. *Educational Forum, 48,* 243–252.

Leonardo, N. (2020). *Active listening techniques: 30 practical tools to hone your communication skills*. Callisto Media.

Patterson, K., Crenny, J., McMillan, R., & Switzler, A. (2011). *Crucial conversations: Tools for talking when stakes are high*. McGraw-Hill Education.

Piaget, J., & Cook, M. T. (1952). *The origins of intelligence in children*. International University Press.

PART III

**HOW CAN I MAKE MY CLASSROOM MANAGEMENT
EFFECTIVE WHILE ENCOURAGING MY STUDENTS
TO BECOME SELF-REGULATING AGENTS
OF THEIR OWN BEHAVIOR?**

CHAPTER 9

TEACHING SELF-RESPECT IS WAY MORE IMPORTANT THAN DEVELOPING POSITIVE SELF-CONCEPTS

It is part of the lore of teaching that unless a child has a positive self-concept, she or he will not be able to learn much in school. This idea has a long history because there is an element of truth in it. People need to feel good about who they are to be fully functioning individuals. But unfortunately, this notion has often led to vapid activities designed to build up self-esteem by proclaiming to children that they are special. Too many times, commercial materials, canned programs, and teacher-developed activities have focused on helping students feel good about themselves without giving them any substantial reason for doing so. That may sound like I am being cold-hearted, but my experience is that students, even young students, know when they are being conned. They know when they are struggling academically, socially, or emotionally; and filling out a worksheet, writing a haiku, or making a photo album will not do much to change how they are feeling about themselves in the long run.

This chapter argues that giving them opportunities to earn self-respect in school is much smarter and better for the students than focusing on a shallow notion of self-concept enhancement. "Self-respect" in this context is something individuals earn when they accomplish difficult tasks that they and those they care about see as valuable. There is no need for

Teaching as a Human Activity: Ways to Make Classrooms Joyful and Effective
pp. 77–84
Copyright © 2021 by Information Age Publishing

empty praise or condescending congratulations; students know that they have accomplished worthy tasks, and they think differently about their capabilities when they have real evidence that their hard work has paid off.

Classrooms in which the development of self-respect is central shift students' focus away from doing whatever each individual needs to do to draw attention to themselves (in positive and negative ways) to putting energy into monitoring and improving their own capabilities as young people and learners. Classrooms are ideal places for developing a sense of self-respect. When students are given difficult assignments that they see as meaningful and important and they receive the support they need to accomplish those tasks, a healthy sense of self-respect can be the outcome. Examples are spelled out in this chapter.

As an undergraduate majoring in political science at the University of Utah, I really did not know where my life was headed. I had just been discharged after serving two years in the army. I loved going to school and had a vague idea that I would go to law school or join the diplomatic corps—but that never felt like a real plan. I took a summer course from the College of Education that sent students to visit a variety of educational institutions that were open during the summer. We went to Job Corps sites, summer school classrooms, and a Head Start Center in the heart of Salt Lake City. Sitting in the back of the 3-year-old class at the Head Start, I had an epiphanic moment that changed my life. A tiny girl with the sweetest eyes I have ever seen got up from her place on the circle, walked back to me, and raised her arms to be picked up. That was it! I started spending all my free time volunteering at the center, changed my major, and implemented a real plan for my future—I was going to be a Head Start teacher.

Because it would have added more than a year to my time in school to earn a degree in early childhood education, I opted for an elementary education major. As mentioned in other places in this book, the education programs at Utah were heavily influenced by the progressive educators and influential psychologists of the day. We read folks like John Holt, Rollo May, Ivan Illich, A. S. Neill, Herb Cole, Abraham Maslow, Carl Rogers, and Art Combs. Phenomenological psychology provided the theoretical doctrine at the base of our studies, and I was a total convert. I later moved to the state of Florida so I could establish residency, do a PhD at the University of Florida, and study with Combs (who actually moved to another university before I enrolled).

Long way around to say that I was thoroughly into the tenets of self-concept development and self-actualization that permeated phenomenological thinking. These ideas had a powerful influence on my teaching and my personal life. When prompted by a professor to introduce ourselves and name our goals for the next five years, I recall announcing to my master's degree peers at the University of North Florida that I wanted to become more fully self-actualized. Lord, that sounds self-righteous, self-centered, and self-serving now—and it was. I was a flag bearer for what came to be called the "me generation." My obsession with fulfilling my *self* turned out to be hurtful to lots of other adults during that part of my life. These ideas formed the core of my teaching beliefs, but I do not think the elementary school students I taught in Kansas City and Jacksonville were damaged in any significant way. It took a while, but I figured out along the way that earning self-respect was a much better goal than inflating one's self-esteem.

Summarizing his analysis of the relationship between self-concept and learning, one scholar from the 1960s wrote, "The Self is an essential aspect of the learning process and so is of primary concern to those interested in any way in the growth of children" (Staines, 1963, p. 104). That the word "Self" was capitalized in the original says a lot. The notion that having a positive self-concept is vital to learning did not disappear with the passing of the me generation. It remains a staple in scholarly articles (e.g., Craven & Marsh, 2008) and educational psychology textbooks (e.g., Woolfolk, 2012). And the idea that students need to feel good about themselves in order to be successful makes sense; but the rub comes when school and commercial curricula and teacher efforts are so focused on the *feel good* part that they forget the *successful* bit. For me, that is where self-respect is a much more powerful construct for improving kids' lives than self-concept.

I began to think about the differences between self-respect and self-concept after reading John Rawls' (1971) landmark philosophical treatise, *A Theory of Justice*. Of course, Rawls was not making any comparisons to tenets of self-psychology; but for me the contrasts are striking. Rawls argued that self-respect is not something people are born with, but has to be learned and developed over time. It is learned from the experience of taking on difficult tasks that you and those around you see as important and successfully accomplishing those tasks. Self-respect is earned, not conferred. Rawls saw schools (along with other basic institutions—like the family) as being responsible for teaching self-respect. And he thought that learning self-respect was vital for individuals and for the health of society at large. He wrote that self-respect is "essential if citizens are to have a lively sense of their own worth as moral persons" (p. 256), adding,

> Without self respect nothing may seem worth doing.... All desire and activity becomes empty and vain, and we sink into apathy and cynicism. If we do not have a secure sense of self-respect, then we will no longer see our ends and aims as worth pursuing; they will cease to be of value to us. (p. 386)

If Rawls is even partly right about the impact of not developing a secure sense of self-respect, then as educators, we should be doing much more to support children and young people's efforts to learn to respect themselves for what they are capable of accomplishing. If families and other societal institutions are failing to teach self-respect to the next generation, then all the more reason that schools should make this a priority. So how is self-respect different from self-esteem?

It is possible for someone to have a highly developed positive self-concept without having anything substantial to back up that perception. We have all observed people (some in high places) who "are often wrong but never in doubt." Their inflated view of themselves turns out to get in the way of their actually learning what they need to know to make good decisions or keeps them from listening to others who actually know something about the issues at hand. Of course, having a positive self-image is not inherently bad; but it can mask ignorance and instability if it is not supported with evidence of competence and accomplishment. The latter is what a focus on self-respect can provide.

Self-respect is learned within a context of challenge, effort, and achievement. It is not bestowed by loving parents, caring pastors, or kindly teachers; it is earned by individuals who take on difficult tasks and reap evidence of their accomplishments. My youngest granddaughter was part of young people's theater group that was preparing to stage *The Jungle Book*. Although she was only five and one of youngest in the troupe, she wanted to try out for a leading role (Shanti), which involved many lines and lots of singing. She worked with the leaders of the theater group and spent extra hours at home learning lines and perfecting her singing to prepare for the audition. Parents were not allowed in the auditions, but when she came out, she proclaimed, "I did it!" She did not say, "I got the part" because she did not know the outcome; but she knew she had faced a difficult challenge, done her best to prepare, and had performed well under pressure. For me, "I did it" did not mean "I am special;" it meant "I can do difficult stuff." Blair did win the part, and her self-respect was further enhanced as she demonstrated her skills and composure during the play's performances.

What I am calling for here is for students to come away from school experiences with the sense that, "I am empowered," rather than internalizing the notion that, "I am entitled." I am afraid that an emphasis on making kids feel special and unique leads too many kids to see themselves as superior and deserving. Providing learning experiences and an environment that teaches self-respect gives young people the chance to experience the benefits of hard work and celebrate the powerful feelings that come with accomplishing difficult tasks. Deep down, kids know when they have earned self-respect; and they know when they are being flimflammed with activities that have no observable purpose beyond boosting their egos.

Self-concept development in school has generated a significant body of research. It is pretty clear that there are strong positive correlations between self-concepts and achievement (Huitt, 2009); but as the old axiom goes, "correlation does not imply causation." In this context, that means that just because achievement scores are higher in kids with high self-concept scores does not automatically tell us that having a higher self-concept causes higher achievement. It is possible that higher achievement leads to higher self-concepts or that an additional factor or factors (e.g., having a great teacher or well-educated parents) caused both self-concept and achievement to be higher. Some scholars who have studied these relationships have concluded that it is actually more likely that high achievement leads to higher self-concepts than the inverse. Gage and Berliner (1992) summarize:

> The evidence is accumulating to indicate that level of school success, particularly over many years, predicts level of regard of self and one's own ability; whereas level of self-esteem does not predict level of school achievement. The implication is that teachers need to concentrate on the academic successes and failures of their students. It is the students' history of success and failure that gives them the information with which to assess themselves. (p. 159)

This critique of the impact of self-concept on achievement fits with the thesis of this chapter; that is, it makes more sense to put our energies into teaching self-respect than promoting self-concept development for its own sake.

So what does self-respect look like in classrooms and how can teachers do a better job of teaching it? First of all, the ethos that permeates the classroom challenges individuals to do their best. It is not about beating your classmates or chasing some arbitrary standard set by unseen others. Teachers expect their charges to put forth their best effort, they expect to work beside students in order for them to accomplish difficult tasks, and they expect continuous progress. It is the effort, the support, and the progress that define what is important in classrooms where students learn self-respect.

I admire Olympic athletes who proudly represent their countries in events in which they have little or no chance of winning a medal. They work just as hard as the elite performers in their sports and take great satisfaction in participating. In interviews, they often describe how proud they are to have accomplished their "personal best." They do not have to stand on the winners' podium to feel self-respect; they have earned that sense of accomplishment from doing their level best to be all they can be.

It is that feeling that teachers can instill in children when they set up classrooms that teach self-respect. Young people can learn that *personal best* will look different for different individuals and that there is great pride to be earned from taking on difficult challenges and working hard to meet them.

Expecting and rewarding best effort sometimes flies in the face of the official reward systems in schools. Too often for too many kids, arbitrary standards are in place, and students who do not meet those standards (as assessed on standardized tests) are officially labeled as deficient. They are identified as "at risk," they are placed in remedial programs, their curriculum is narrowed to focus on areas of weakness, they are retained in grade level, they are tracked into tiered systems of secondary education that limit their life chances, and they internalize the stigma of being perceived by the system as *less than normal* (Hatch, 2015; Jackson, 2013; Strauss, 2019). Faced with what they see as the impossibility of succeeding when the cards are stacked against them, too many students stop trying—a phenomenon often referred to as "learned helplessness."

According to the American Psychological Association (2020), learned helplessness occurs when someone repeatedly faces uncontrollable, stressful situations, then does not exercise control when it becomes available. For kids in school, this translates to, "No matter how hard I try, I will always be found lacking, so why would I keep butting my head against the wall?" If striving for individual best performance is the norm in classrooms, students have a way to counter feelings of learned helplessness if they are experiencing them. Better, these feelings need never arise in school if kids are measured against goals that are developed with a commitment to constant improvement and assessed in ways that document students' hard work and demonstrate their progress.

In classrooms that teach self-respect, teachers help students set high but achievable goals. They signal students that nothing but their best effort will do and then make sure that individual personal bests are supported, recognized, and rewarded. Children and young people learn that they have control over their learning; they develop a secure sense that they are capable of learning important stuff; they get lots of feedback that tells them they are worthy of respect because they can do difficult things; and they learn to self-monitor and self-evaluate so that they do not depend on the assessments of others (or the system) to know that they are working hard and moving forward.

The support part is critical here. Just saying you expect everyone to go for their personal best will not be sufficient to convince young learners that they are worthy of self-respect. They have to be given tasks that they see as difficult and worth doing (not "baby work" or "dumbbell assignments"). They have to take action and be responsible for their effort (you cannot do it for them). They need to have their efforts scaffolded by someone who knows how to successfully complete the tasks (usually the teacher, but not always). They need to have the scaffolding reduced so that they can see that they have put forth the effort required to master the material themselves (see Chapter 13). And, they need opportunities to reflect on the process and celebrate the sense of self-respect that comes with it (i.e., "I did it!").

This takes me back to Blair's feeling of self-respect when she came out of her audition for the *Jungle Book*. My granddaughter wanted to try out for a part with lots of lines and solos, even though she realized that it would require tons of practice (and no guarantee of getting the role). It was a tough ask, but she wanted to try. Her older sister (also in the play), her mother, and especially her father spent hours upon hours feeding Blair her lines, singing the chorus parts of her songs, and encouraging her to be natural and project her voice. Their support helped get her to the place where she was confidant going into the audition. She could not have done it without them; but 5-year-old Blair did the hard work, and she earned the feeling of accomplishment that went with doing her very best.

As a teacher, you will have lots of options regarding what you will do and how you will do it in the classroom. Of course, you want your students to have a healthy self-concept. It is awful to think about adults who are so insecure themselves that they say and do things that damage young peoples' views of themselves. A caring teacher would never do that, but here is a way to systematically do the opposite. Intentionally teaching in ways that empower students and develop self-respect provides an approach that can have it both ways. Yes, we want to improve our students' feelings about themselves, but let's give them something substantial to feel good about. Let's give them difficult tasks, support them as they do their best, and celebrate with them as they see how capable they are. Let's make teaching self-respect a core value in our classrooms.

REFERENCES

American Psychological Association. (2020). Learned helplessness. *APA Dictionary of Psychology*. https://dictionary.apa.org/learned-helplessness

Craven, R. G., & Marsh, H. W. (2008). The centrality of the self-concept construct for psychological wellbeing and unlocking human potential: Implications for child and educational psychologists. *Educational and Child Psychology, 25*(2), 104–118.

Gage, N., & Berliner, D. (1992). *Educational psychology* (5th ed.). Houghton Mifflin.

Hatch, J. A. (2015). *Reclaiming the teaching profession: Transforming the dialogue on public education*. Roman and Littlefield.

Huitt, W. (2009). Self-concept and self-esteem. *Educational Psychology Interactive*. http://www.edpsycinteractive.org/topics/regsys/self.html

Jackson, J. (2013, May 30). Pivoting from standards- to supports-based reform. *Education Week*. http://www.*edweek*.org/ew/articles/2013/05/08/30jackson .h32.html

Rawls, J. (1971). *A theory of justice*. Harvard University Press.

Staines, J. W. (1963). The self-concept in learning and teaching. *Australian Journal of Education, 7*(3), 104–118.

Strauss, V. (2019, January 23). Why we should stop labeling students as 'at risk'— And the best alternative. *Washington Post*. https://www.washingtonpost.com/ education/2019/01/23/why-we-should-stop-labeling-students-risk-best-alternative/

Woolfolk, A. (2012). *Educational psychology* (12th ed.). Pearson.

CHAPTER 10

TEACHERS NEED TO MAKE RULES THAT MAKE SENSE AND REFLECT THE GENUINE PURPOSES OF THE CLASSROOM

For me, our adversarial judicial system is a mess. In the United States, the search for justice is not the primary aim of the court system. Because of how we have decided to adjudicate criminal and civil cases, being innocent or guilty is not nearly as important as how effective your lawyer is at arguing your case. In our system, law breakers and cheats who can afford the "best" representation in court have a way better chance of coming out on top. We have all seen cases where powerful, high-profile people have gotten away with murder (literally and figuratively). We seem to just accept that the system is rigged, looking the other way when people without resources get hammered, while those with wealth and influence get over.

But our adversarial model is not the only way to structure a legal system for deciding what is right and wrong. For example, France and Germany operate under an inquisitorial system, in which the court actively investigates the facts of the case rather than listening to opposing sides present their version of the truth. Neither approach provides a guarantee of justice, but the adversarial mode perpetuates the point of view that you

Teaching as a Human Activity: Ways to Make Classrooms Joyful and Effective
pp. 85–93
Copyright © 2021 by Information Age Publishing

are only guilty or liable if you lose in court. For me, this mindset reduces personal responsibility to the lowest levels of moral development, as in, "I have done nothing wrong so long as I can weasel my way out of it."

But this is a book about teaching, and you do not need a rant or a civics lesson. What I am after in this chapter is a way to counter the mindset I am describing above. Even if our society seems to be locked into a system of distributing justice that is unequal and unfair, does not mean that children and young people cannot experience ways of dealing with issues of right and wrong that appeal to a higher level of moral reasoning than what they observe around them. They can learn that there are good reasons for having rules and doing what is right. They can learn that they have a responsibility to take the needs of others into account as they make decisions about how they will act. They can learn that there are more good reasons for doing the right thing than lame excuses for doing the self-serving thing. One way to help kids learn these powerful lessons is set up rules that make sense because they are based on a classroom purpose that is shared by everyone.

Part of being a fully functioning human being is having a moral center. Every normally developing individual has a set of core beliefs about right and wrong that guides how they live their lives. Sociopaths are thought to have no conscience and psychopaths manipulate their definition of what is right and wrong to suit their needs (Bonn, 2018); but most people develop some kind of moral sensibility as they progress through childhood and early adulthood. While young people's moral development is influenced by experiences with family, church, and other institutions, schools have a major role to play as well.

As teachers, we have the opportunity to provide models of moral behavior and to set up classrooms in ways that improve students' chances of developing a moral compass that can guide their thinking about right and wrong and enhance their ability to make good decisions about how they will act in the world. I am arguing here that the way you establish and utilize classroom rules can have a positive impact on children's moral development.

The field of moral development research and theorizing has it roots in the work of Lawrence Kohlberg (1981) and has been expanded by scholars like Carole Gilligan (1989) and James Rest (1986). I will use Kohlberg's stage model to demonstrate the general notion that moral understanding follows a predictable path of development that is influenced by people's experiences in school and out. The following is adapted from Evans and colleagues' (2010) summary of Kohlberg's three levels and six stages of moral development:

- Level 1 (Preconventional):

  o Stage 1: Heteronomous morality—individuals justify actions based on avoidance of punishment and the superior power of authorities;

  o Stage 2: Individualistic, instrumental morality—individuals follow rules if it is in their interest to do so;

- Level 2 (Conventional):

  o Stage 3: Interpersonally normative morality—right is defined as meeting the expectations of those to whom one is close and carrying out appropriate, acceptable social roles;

  o Stage 4: Social system morality—individuals behave in a way that maintains the system and fulfills societal obligations;

- Level 3 (Postconventional or Principled):

  o Stage 5: Human rights and social welfare morality—laws and societal systems are evaluated based on the extent to which they promote fundamental human rights and values; and

  o Stage 6: Morality of universalizable, reversible, and prescriptive general ethical principles—decisions are based on universal generalizable principles that apply in all situations.

The track to moral maturity in this model travels from the belief that one is guilty only if caught and punished through a level of believing that one has an obligation to do what is right to preserve the rights of others to a place where one is applying universal ethical principles to decide what is right and wrong. My view is that most of U.S. society is stuck at Level 1 of moral development—if we can avoid punishment and pick and chose which rules serve our purposes, all is right with the world. I would like to see young people move at least to Level 2 thinking as a result of experiences in school—so they think it is right to behave in ways that take into account the needs of those around them, thus serving to enhance the cohesion of the group. Getting kids to this level creates the opportunity for them to approach Level 3 moral thinking—wherein they can make decisions based on fundamental human rights and values.

I think we can all agree that classroom rules are essential to a smooth-running classroom. Kids need to know what is expected of them at school or they will be constantly trying to find the limits of what they can get away with. But for my money, some kinds of rules are better than others. There are rules about rules that have been around teaching for a long time. Some of these make perfect sense, but some may actually hurt the chances that rules will be effective. I want to explore and debunk some of these notions of how rules should be generated, stated, and put into action, suggesting that a few general rules established by the teacher and based on genuine purposes that permeate the classroom will work best day to day as well as support the overall moral development of students. Examples from real classrooms and a discussion of how to implement such an approach conclude this chapter.

One of the most common suggestions for establishing rules is to let students participate in designing rules and consequences for classroom behavior. The upside of this approach is that the kids own the rules and are therefore more committed to them than if they are handed down by the teacher. This process seems more democratic in that it encourages participation in decision making that impacts the classroom society. I get that these are positive outcomes if everything goes well; but, there are lots of places where student participation in rule making can go wrong.

Especially with younger learners, teachers have to guide the process of establishing rules. Teachers set parameters, prescribe steps, and direct the discussions for rule generation; otherwise, it would be a free-for-all. Lots of times, teachers provide so much "guidance" that everyone involved knows where the rules really came from. Teachers know what kinds of behaviors need to be included and what kinds do not, so they lead discussions with questions or other rhetorical devices to shape the final product. Kids can see what kinds of suggestions end up on the whiteboard and which ones are questioned, challenged, or ignored.

In other settings, children are given less guidance and end up setting up long lists of expectations and consequences that try to cover every eventuality imaginable. This can happen with teacher-produced rules as well. With this approach, a long laundry list of do nots is usually produced, along with designated consequences for each infraction (and it is part of teacher lore that student generated consequences are more punitive than those of teachers). In my mind, this approach mirrors society's system of laws and punishments and in doing so encourages the kind of low-level moral reasoning discussed above. Classroom rules are so specific that operating in the classroom becomes a game of finding loopholes and skirting the letter of the law. Kids are socialized into operating at Level 1 of moral development (Evans et al., 2010; Kohlberg, 1989). They learn that not getting caught is the goal and that rules can be manipulated to suit their personal impulses and desires.

Another rule for making rules that many teachers have been taught is that classroom rules should be stated in positive terms. Rather than specifying what students cannot do, rules should be written as affirmatives. For example, you would not have a rule that says you cannot interrupt others (including the teacher) when they are talking; but you might include something like, "You will be a good listener at all times." I accept that the tone of the affirmative approach is better than a long list of negatives for students to avoid. However, I worry that in practice, the distinction between framing the rules as do nots versus dos may be moot. It all depends on how the students perceive what is going on. If they still think of the rules as something to be skirted, manipulated, or disputed, then they are learning the same moral lessons either way.

Another trend that comes and goes in education is the adoption of system- or schoolwide discipline plans that have been produced and sold by outside vendors. These plans virtually always include a set of strictly defined rules and clearly prescribed consequences for breaking them. They are often based on the assumption that if rules are clear and students violate them, then consequences should be automatic. This is supposed to put responsibility on kids and take decisions about whom and what behavior to punish out of the teachers' hands. These packaged programs are often adopted by urban schools and other institutions that serve students with high needs. While some of these discipline systems have elements on their face that are attractive to me (e.g., an emphasis on building character), most mirror closely the structure of the U.S. system of criminal justice, thus teaching students that avoiding punishment is the ultimate aim. Further, it places teachers in the role of police officers whose job it is to enforce laws made by invisible others.

I think we can do better. Another way of thinking about rules is for the teacher to create three or four basic rules that directly reflect the purposes of the classroom. The combination of four elements makes this way of establishing rules different from those used in most schoolrooms. These elements are: (1) Rules are few in number; (2) They are general in nature; (3) They are put forth by the teacher; and (4) Rules are directly tied to the established purposes of the classroom. Each element is important, but the last is critical.

First, you only need three or four rules. The goal is for young people to internalize their responsibility for doing what is right. If you have a long list of rules, you invite students to respond to being called out for obviously inappropriate behavior with, "But there is no rule that says I cannot do that!" For the same reasons, you want general rules that expect children to make moral judgments about their behavior instead of trying to con their way out of taking responsibility, arguing for example, "Emily did not get in trouble when she did the same thing yesterday!" And, I think it is the teacher's job to create the rules and share them with the students. These rules are too vital to how the year is going to progress to go through a process (often a charade) through which students develop their own rules. If the rules make sense, are closely linked to the kids' and teachers' purpose for being there, then students will take ownership of them and see them as necessary and fair.

I devoted an entire chapter to the importance of having a shared purpose in your classroom (see Chapter 2). The whole point of having rules is to maintain an environment in which no one is threatened and everyone thrives. Kids need a reason to behave that goes beyond avoiding getting caught. The goal is for students to take responsibility for their own behavior because not doing so hurts the chances of others to accomplish the shared aims of the community. I argued in Chapter 2 that most students (and too many teachers) do not have a clear idea of why they are in school. Having a set of arbitrary rules based on the superior power of the teacher and the need for the system to control student behavior reinforces kids' perceptions that schools are institutions designed to manage rather than teach them. Having a shared and meaningful purpose, classrooms can become places where individuals work as a team to accomplish important aims. Providing a few general rules that make that purpose come to life can help support young people's success in school and advance their developing moral sensibilities.

I want to provide one detailed description of this approach to classroom rule making from my own early childhood teaching, then project how it might look in other classrooms at different levels. As briefly mentioned in earlier chapters, I taught kindergarten in Jacksonville, Florida. In this classroom, our purpose was captured in a bulletin board that said, "Learn a little every day!" We called ourselves the K Team, and we lived the idea that the reason we were there together was to learn. Learning was our purpose, and everything we did came back to this definitional characteristic.

I used the Jacksonville example in a 2005 book about kindergarten teaching. The rules in this classroom were part and parcel of our purpose. Our classroom rules helped us focus ourselves on making sure everyone was a successful member of our learning team. Our three rules were:

- We are the K Team, and we are here to learn;
- We learn best when we feel safe and happy; and
- We will help each other learn a little every day.

In early childhood classrooms, it is essential to go over the rules early and often; but it is important in any setting to post the rules in a prominent place and frequently remind students of their importance and what they mean in practice. This can be done by giving examples or getting students to role-play situations that connect rules to specific student behavior. So for our K Team, I might prompt, "When you are wandering around the room, are you learning?" or "When you do something to make others feel afraid or sad, are you helping them learn?"

I summarized the value of having a few general rules in the kindergarten teaching book:

> But the real power of these simple rules is in redirecting children's behavior. At this point the rules come to life for children. When one child is intimidating another either physically or verbally, the rules make it clear that someone else's chances to learn are jeopardized. A rule that says that everyone must have every chance to learn is much different than a rule that says no hitting or no threatening. In the case of the latter, the teacher becomes the police officer and judge, and the child's reason for not hitting or threatening is to avoid getting caught. (Hatch, 2005, p. 114)

The whole point of any classroom management system ought to be to help students learn to manage their own behavior, otherwise we are replicating the criminal justice system and perpetuating a low level of moral development. When there are good reasons for choosing to do the right thing, children and young people can internalize a moral mindset that includes consideration of others and valuing the needs of the group. Having a shared purpose for being there, a *raison d'etre*, provides the basis for establishing rules that build cohesion and cooperation and minimize disruptions and discord. In the next paragraphs, I will offer some examples of rules that might be generated by teachers who are focused on classroom purposes other than learning.

In Chapter 2, which is all about the importance of establishing classroom purposes, three exemplary options are described. Again, these are not the only worthy choices—they are just possible purposes; and those suggested here are not the only rules that could fit these purposes. The goal is to get you thinking about how to frame rules that will make sense given your purposes, whatever they turn out to be. For balance, I will frame the examples as if they were for upper elementary, middle school, and high school classrooms.

Cooperation could be the defining purpose of an upper elementary classroom. As described in Chapter 2, cooperation is undervalued in school and society and, in contrast with our obsession with competition and winning at any cost, could provide a meaningful purpose for school experiences. Potential rules in a classroom based on cooperation might look like guidelines that have been developed by advocates for a cooperative learning approach (e.g., Gillies, 2007; Schul, 2012):

- Show respect for others' efforts and opinions;
- Stay engaged and give your best effort; and
- Help each other and support the team.

Maximizing individual capabilities is a purpose that could be adopted at the middle school level. If the shared goal is to ensure that every individual has the opportunity to become all he or she can be, then we need to set up classrooms that address the strengths and needs of the whole child. That means meeting children as complex human beings, as "capacities rather than commodities" (Buzzelli, 2020, p. 168). Possible rules could include:

- Respect differences and celebrate unique contributions;
- Support everyone's right to be themselves; and
- Help maintain an atmosphere in which everyone can fulfill their potential.

Educating for a democracy of the intellect is the third purpose outlined in Chapter 2. It could be a fitting purpose in high school and it could give young people the chance to move to Level 3 of moral reasoning, in which they apply universal principles to their decision making. When focused on a democracy of the intellect, classrooms become places where students are expected to be responsible participants in making things work. They are taught the importance of applying "informed integrity" as citizens of the classroom and the world (Hatch & Conrath, 1988, p. 44). That means that they need to have the intellectual tools to sift through extraneous and deceptive information and the will to stand up for what is right. I can picture rules like the following in classrooms that emphasize educating for a democracy of the intellect:

- Make sound decisions based on solid understanding;
- Work with others to improve the classroom climate; and
- Always do the right thing.

Rules are essential in schools and society. But rules for classrooms do not have to perpetuate the mindset in children and young people that rules are arbitrary standards that people with power impose on those with less. We can establish rules that actually make sense—to students and teachers—because following them makes it possible to achieve the shared purposes of the group. Kids need to see a genuine purpose for being in school, and that purpose can come to life when right kind of classroom rules are in place. Setting, teaching, and consistently applying purpose-based rules make classrooms run more smoothly and give young people the chance to advance their moral development. At the least, we can move them beyond doing what is necessary to avoid punishment in the direction of making decisions for the good of the whole. With effort and consistency, we can do more, introducing the possibility of making moral decisions based on principles like personal integrity, universal justice, and treating others as you would like to be treated. We need this kind of moral improvement in school and society.

REFERENCES

Bonn, S. A. (2018, January 9). The differences between psychopaths and sociopaths. *Psychology Today*, https://www.psychologytoday.com/us/blog/wicked-deeds/201801/the-differences-between-psychopaths-and-sociopaths

Buzzelli, C. A. (2020). Changing the discourse: The capability approach and early childhood education. In J. J. Mueller & N. File (Eds.), *Curriculum in early childhood education: Re-examined, reclaimed, renewed* (pp. 161–176). Routledge.

Evans, N. J., Forney, D. S., Guido, F. M., Patton, L. D., & Renn, K. A. (2010). *Student development in college: Theory, research, and practice* (2nd ed.). Jossey-Bass.

Gillies, R. (2007). *Cooperative learning: Integrating theory and practice*. SAGE.

Gilligan, C. (1989). *Mapping the moral domain: A contribution to women's thinking to psychological theory and education*. Harvard University Press.

Hatch, J. A. (2005). *Teaching in the new kindergarten*. Delmar.

Hatch, J. A., & Conrath, J. M. (1988). Refocusing the identity of schooling: Education for a democracy of the intellect. *Kappa Delta Pi Record, 24*(1), 41–45.

Kohlberg, L. (1981). *The philosophy of moral development: Moral stages and the idea of justice*. Harper & Row.

Rest, J. R. (1986). *Moral development: Advances in research and theory*. Praeger.

Schul, J. E. (2012). Revisiting an old friend: The practice and promise of cooperative learning for the twenty-first century. *The Social Studies, 102*, 88–93.

CHAPTER 11

WHEN TEACHERS GET IN POWER STRUGGLES WITH STUDENTS, WE LOSE EVERY TIME

When I think back on my years as a public school teacher, I remember my failures as much as my successes—maybe more. That probably says more about me than about teaching. I did not start my career with the aim of creating classroom communities in which humanity could be valued, expressed, and nurtured; but I have always recognized the central importance of human emotions in the teaching and learning process. I came to teaching late in my university studies, and I came because I cared about kids and wanted desperately to make a positive difference in their lives and in the world we shared.

Some of my most vivid fails as a teacher happened when my own shortcomings or the difficulties faced by my students or the institutional pressures of the places where I worked got the best of me. Failures that stand out in retrospect are times when my personal and professional commitments were overridden by my reaction to the circumstances of the moment. After 2 years teaching in Kansas City, Missouri, I moved to Jacksonville, Florida. I was hired to teach a fourth grade class in a newly desegregated school in Jacksonville's city center. The class to which I was assigned had run off their first teacher a few days into the school year—in fact, she somehow sustained a broken arm and refused to come back. The class had a reputation as the "bad kids," and they knew it.

Teaching as a Human Activity: Ways to Make Classrooms Joyful and Effective
pp. 95–101
Copyright © 2021 by Information Age Publishing

I was coming from a wonderful experience teaching in an all-Black school in inner-city Kansas City. I was confident that I could work with all the kids, and I was sure the students would see how much I cared and that we could build a new reputation together. Not so much. From my perspective at the time, the students who were most troublesome seemed to read my commitment to caring as weakness. It was only the second year of implementing a desegregation order, and there was ongoing and deep-seated conflict between the White and Black students in the class (and across the school); and although we did experience some genuine success over that first year in coming together as a class, the cross-racial tension seemed always to be there.

I took small groups of my students to Jacksonville Beach (some had never been), organized a party at my apartment (with the help of my girl-friend at the time), and did home visits (which no one at the school had ever done). Still, there was tension in the classroom that made me dread going to work every day and hurt everyone's chances of learning. When portraying myself as a caring teacher was not enough to dampen the antagonism in the room, I made a strategic failure: I decided I would show them who was boss and clamp down on all the defiance, disruptions and misbehavior. I set myself up for a battle I could not win. I did and said things during those few months in Jacksonville that I count as the worst mistakes of my career.

I remembered advice I had received somewhere in my training that to get a classroom under control, I should pick out the worst offenders and focus on bringing them into line—the logic being that others would follow. The leading offenders in this fourth grade were two Black 10-year-old boys whose reputation for being bad was known throughout the school and across the subsidized housing community in which they lived. They "boosted" lunch money from other kids, cut the upholstery in my car while being transported from the party at my apartment, and jumped on the sink in the boys' bathroom until it came off the wall. They were way tougher than I was, and getting them "in line" was not going to work out.

I was loud. I was physical. I was sarcastic. I was punitive. I was uncompromising. I was harsh. I was going to show them I was in charge. I failed. Living with my failure, I became super deflated and seriously depressed. I was unhappy with what I was doing and hated what I was becoming. I even looked into quitting that teaching job and going to work at Head Start; but the Head Start program in Jacksonville was not at the same place as the one in Salt Lake City, where I fell in love with teaching.

Finally, I went to my principal asking for help. The first thing she did was arrange coverage for my room so I could spend time observing one of my fourth grade colleagues as she taught. I remember marveling at how smoothly her day ran. Her students knew exactly what to do and they did it with little or no prompting. They were not perfect, but all their teacher had to do was give them a look (we called it "cutting her eyes" back in the day) and they got back on track. I was stunned and embarrassed. Here was this fragile looking Black woman with a cane who had perfect control, while I could barely get through the day without some kind of dramatic encounter. Worse, it appeared that she maintained a smooth running classroom with little or no visible effort.

This great teacher and I had one of the most important talks of my career standing in the breezeway outside her classroom after one of my observations. I remember her asking, "What have you won if you come out on top in a battle with a 10-year-old?" She was trying to help me see that you are an automatic loser if you let yourself get drawn into a power struggle with your students. The risks are great that you will lose the confrontation, thus reinforcing the resistant stance of your antagonist in front of everyone present. But even if you win, you come off as an adult who has to use his superior size or position to dominate a child. I am not the first professional to advice against getting into power struggles with kids (e.g., McNeely, 2020), but I can attest from experience that they never work out.

As a teacher who has taught from kindergarten through doctoral studies, my advice is to avoid power struggles at all cost. As a parent of two boys who are now successful adults, my advice is the same. It is especially important for teachers because classrooms are fishbowls in which every interaction teachers have with their students is observed by everyone present. Some students become adept at drawing teachers into conflicts that can lead to a win or a loss for the teacher. Once inside one of these power struggles, teachers feel like they have to win—no matter the cost. Problem is, like my mentor in Jacksonville taught me, what have you really won if you somehow manage to come out on top?

What most often happens is that everyone sees that the teacher is able to be manipulated by the student. When students learn what gets to their teacher, the chances that those same buttons will be pushed again go way up. When you set up your classroom as a battleground, like I did in Florida, you are consigning yourself to constant struggle. Every interaction becomes a possible source of conflict, and the negative vibe in the room overwhelms the good feelings that go with learning important stuff and sharing personal and academic success with those around you.

This kind of situation is terrible for you and not fair to the kids with whom you battle or to the other young people in the room. The answer is to avoid being drawn into these power struggles from the start—to never get to a place where your classroom feels like a battle zone. This chapter describes common traps that teachers often fall into and presents alternative strategies that can reshape interactions between teachers and students so that win or lose confrontations do not arise.

One trap that new teachers often fall prey to parallels what happened to me in Jacksonville. Novice teachers often do not present themselves as competent, capable adults who are there to lead the class. They either come off as wanting to be friends with the students or needing to be in control of them. Neither positioning will work out for the teachers or their students. Each extreme places teachers in a vulnerable spot. Wanting to be pals with students gives them the power to withhold the affection you seek when you have to make tough decisions in the classroom. And trying to be a prison warden sets you up for constant antagonism (and occasional full-blown riots) as your students do everything they can to subvert your power.

Better to show the students that you care by following the advice in the previous chapters on being a warm demander (Chapter 7) and setting up classroom rules that reflect the purposes of your classroom (Chapter 10). Warm demanders show they care by having high expectations and an uncompromising attitude about everyone's responsibility to do their best (Bondy & Ross, 2008; Irvine & Fraser, 1998). If there is a meaningful purpose for being there, then the teacher's rules are in place for a reason, and she does not have to rely on her personal or positional power to enforce them. It is not her against the kids; it is everyone doing what is right for the good of the whole.

Young people want someone to be in charge, so teachers need to project confidence and competence. Students need the sense that their teachers know what they are doing and are there to accomplish important work. When I watched my fourth grade mentor working with her students, I figured out something that became central to my teaching from that point on. In her classroom, it was *unthinkable* to not follow classroom expectations. When someone forgot where he was or acted out or started playing around, this amazing teacher was positively shocked—at least she acted that way. It was like, "Wow, I am so surprised that you would actually do that in here!" She never raised her voice, never showed frustration or anger, never cajoled or threatened; she just cut her eyes in her special way or said something that communicated her surprise, and the students got back on track. I could never duplicate the presence of my colleague, but I have learned to set up classrooms and carry myself in ways that communicated that I was in charge and expectations that everyone had responsibility for the smooth operation of the class were developed to the point that they were taken for granted.

Another trap that new teachers often fall prey to is making threats or setting ultimatums they cannot follow through on. In the heat of the moment, when things are going badly with a class or an individual student, teachers sometimes say foolish things in order to win that moment. Essentially, they are bluffing—coming up with a consequence that they cannot or should not invoke. Like all bluffs, it becomes a disaster when you get called. You did not just lose face in the moment when the students see you will not be able to follow through, you set the stage for the loss of future confrontations because they know you can be exposed as a bluffer. In addition, lots of times when teachers shoot from the hip when promising over-the-top consequences, they shoot themselves in the foot, threatening outcomes that end up punishing themselves as much as their students—as in taking away recess time from elementary students when everyone desperately needs a break.

Better to avoid being drawn into situations in which you are making up punishments in order to coerce students into doing what you want. If things start to escalate to a place where you feel like making idle threats, you need to be the adult in the room and take another tack. Calling a pause or redirecting the interaction are better alternatives than making promises you cannot keep or will regret. If you follow the advice above and throughout this book, being drawn into power struggles should be a rare occurrence; but if things start going that way, it is okay to say something like, "Let's take a minute to think about our rules," or "We need to deal with this later so we can get back to work."

I know the feeling of being drawn into power struggles. It has happened to me teaching in the classroom and raising my sons. Thinking about those times reminds me of something I mentioned in Chapter 6: "You Do Not Have to Be Perfect to Be Good." Sometimes things happen that get under our skin. Sometimes we are tired and on edge, which makes us less likely to have perfect control of our emotions and reactions. We mess up and say stuff we regret—often as soon as it comes out of our mouths. We are not perfect. It is fine to pursue perfection; it is foolish to expect it. But, just because you screw up once in a while does not mean all the other good things you have done do not count. It does not make you any less a person or worthy role model to admit your mistakes; in fact, it elevates your humanness. It gives you credibility as a teacher (or a parent) to apologize and explain how you'll do better in the future.

Another situation with a high degree of risk develops when the teacher finds herself in an ongoing antagonistic relationship with a particular student or two. Above, I described such a relationship with the two boys in my fourth grade; but, I have felt the beginnings of situations like these in interactions younger and older students (even graduate students). I am intentional about using the word "felt" because I have learned to monitor my gut reactions when I sense that I am getting close to responding from a position of presumed superior authority (i.e., being drawn into a power struggle). When those feelings arise, I make myself step back and respond in ways that will help resolve rather than escalate the potential conflict.

I have lots of anecdotal evidence that too many teachers keep up running battles with particular students. When we sent the future educators in our teacher education program into the schools to observe or complete internships, they regularly came back with sad stories of students whom they perceived to be in constant conflict with their teachers. It looked to our preservice teachers like these students could do no right. They were constantly in trouble, and their teachers seemed to be especially tough on them, meting out more and harsher discipline than was received by others in the class. Further, teachers sometimes talked about these students in ways that made it sound like they were the bane of the teachers' existence. It is disingenuous to say that you do not have favorites or to deny that some kids are harder to like than others; but, it borders on educational malpractice to allow problems with particular students to devolve into ongoing antagonisms within which the students have no chance of redemption.

Do not let yourself become a teacher who comes to believe that battling with kids is what you have to do to keep order in school. Do not let yourself get so caught up in winning power struggles at any cost that you forget you are there to provide guidance, experiences, and examples that help young people become successful, well-balanced adults. Do have the capacity to feel yourself being drawn into win or lose conflicts, and do have the restraint to pull back and go another direction. I did not come to teaching (or parenting) with that capacity, and I have lots of regrets. But, I did learn from others and from monitoring myself that I could get better at focusing on finding solutions rather than winning skirmishes.

I have always loved the short story literary genre. One of my personal goals is to read as many great short stories as I can, so I search anthologies and expert lists to figure out what counts as "great." When I started this chapter, I remembered a story by William Carlos Williams (1938) called "The Use of Force." It is one of the shortest stories I have found in this genre, but it is the most powerful description anywhere of what it is like for an adult in authority to be in a power struggle with a child. In this case, the adult is a physician trying to get a young patient to open her mouth so he can diagnose a suspected case of diphtheria. The conflict escalates and soon the doctor becomes more obsessed with dominating this resistant child than caring for her illness or taking into account her age. As the title suggests, force was eventually used by the doctor to complete his diagnosis. I have felt the need to not be defeated by a child that is so vividly portrayed in Williams' story; but I have also learned what I think this author was trying to tell his readers: The use of adult power to dominate children ultimately corrupts the user.

So again, it is a no win situation to get into power struggles with your students. Realizing that it is an automatic lose/lose is the first step, but that is not enough. You need to know yourself well enough to recognize when feelings like those experienced by the doctor in "The Use of Force" story start to arise and know you can halt the escalation of conflict rather than having to admit as the doctor did that his actions "had got beyond reason" (Williams, 1938, p. 2). You can diffuse the potential conflict by redirecting classroom action, taking a pause, or dispassionately applying classroom rules to address the behavior at issue. It is way smarter and way more effective to have established classroom expectations that assume that it is in everyone's best interest to do the right thing than to let yourself be drawn into a standoff that you feel you have to win. Then you can calmly say something like, "Let's remember that we all have a responsibility to do the best we can not to disrupt others' chances to learn" instead of blurting out some idle threat like: "This is the last time you will do that in my classroom!" Fat chance that will work out.

If it is you against them, you will always lose; so do your best to set up classrooms where it is each of us working together for the benefit of all of us. You will never be perfect, but own your mistakes and learn from them. If you start blaming your students for how poorly things are going, step back and take responsibility for making changes to improve relationships in your room. If you feel like quitting, don't. If you feel overwhelmed, get help from your principal, your colleagues, your guidance counselor, and other school staff. Expect of yourself what I hope you expect from your students: to get a little better, smarter, wiser every day.

REFERENCES

Bondy, E., & Ross, D. D. (2008). The teacher as warm demander. *Educational Leadership, 66*(1), 54–58.

Irvine, J. J., & Fraser, J. (1998). Warm demanders: Do national certification standards leave room for the culturally responsive pedagogy of African American teachers? *Education Week, 17*(35), 56.

McNeely, R. (2020). *Avoiding power struggles with students.* National Education Association. http://www.nea.org/tools/49922.htm

Williams, W. C. (1938). The use of force. *Life along the Passaic River.* New Directions.

CHAPTER 12

UNDERSTANDING FACEWORK PRINCIPLES IS ESSENTIAL TO BUILDING POSITIVE CLASSROOM CULTURES

In any social situation, there is "an appreciable chance of being slightly embarrassed or a slight chance of being deeply humiliated" (Goffman, 1959, p. 243). This quote captures the overall theme of the groundbreaking work of Erving Goffman (1959, 1963, 1967, 1971), who studied face-to-face interactions in adults and identified facework principles that undergird how individuals create and protect lines of behavior in social settings. Facework principles are at work in every human interaction. Sometimes called self-presentation, facework starts with the premise that every individual establishes a "face" (a socially constructed identity) that he or she is presenting in a given social setting. Each individual is invested in maintaining his or her face, protecting it from potential threats imposed by others.

In any interaction with another human being, impressions are given off and received, and individuals have a vested interest in controlling the information given off so others will perceive them favorably. Goffman (1959) likens interactions to theater, in which individuals stage performances as social actors. They take lines of behavior, as do the other actors

Teaching as a Human Activity: Ways to Make Classrooms Joyful and Effective
pp. 103–110

in the social interaction. When these lines become suspect because of an embarrassing *gaffe* or *faux pas*, communicative order is disturbed and someone loses face. The brilliance in Goffman's work is in his detailed descriptions of the processes humans utilize to create, protect, maintain, and repair our socially constructed faces.

I believe self-presentation principles can teach teachers a lot about what is going on when they interact with their students. While facework has an inescapable influence on all human interactions, including those in school, they are almost never brought into our conscious awareness. We have internalized the need for and the means to present ourselves in ways that preserve the faces we have created. But, becoming aware of facework processes can help us understand the dynamics of teacher-student interactions in a new way and give us tools for making our interactions with students less threatening and more rewarding for everyone concerned.

One overriding facework concept is that every interaction has a substantive dimension (the content of what is being said) and a ceremonial dimension (what the interaction is saying about how the participants see and value each other's respective faces) (Goffman, 1967). So the way that teachers look at students, the way we stand in relation to them, the tone of voice we use, our choice of words, all send messages that go much deeper than the surface meanings we are trying to convey. Learning to recognize, monitor, and adjust our ceremonial communications in the classroom could go a long way to improving face-to-face interactions in school. This chapter explores this and other basic facework concepts and provides example scenarios demonstrating how these might be effectively applied in real classrooms, especially in situations in which conflicts might arise.

I fell in love with Goffman's books when I was preparing to do my doctoral dissertation at the University of Florida. I had done a pilot study of children's face-to-face interactions with their kindergarten peers and was looking for empirical and theoretical literature that would help me understand what these 5- and 6-year-olds were experiencing during their peer interactions in school. Goffman's insights into how adults work together to stage social performances gave me a set of conceptual tools that helped me analyze and interpret the qualitative field-note data collected for the pilot and my eventual dissertation (Hatch, 1984). I used other theoretical frameworks as well for the dissertation analysis; but I was so impacted by the power of the facework theoretical framework that I did a separate analysis to gage how young kids in both data sets utilized self-presentation in their peer interactions (Hatch, 1987). In fact, I became so engrossed in reading Erving Goffman and understanding facework in action that my grad school friends started calling me "Erv Junior."

The main point of this early thread of my research career was that children were learning and using facework principles in their interactions with each other. Goffman (1963) called children "communication delinquents" because they often violate the rules of adult interaction. My studies (Hatch, 1984, 1987, 1994) showed that even young children utilize many impression management strategies at a rudimentary level and that they are adept at using some strategies in ways that mirrored adult facework. More recent work by scholars studying facework processes in classrooms of older students show that children and young adults can and do use impression management strategies in their social interactions with each other and their teachers, for example, Baiocchi-Wagner (2011) and Payne-Woolridge, 2010). My scholarly agenda took me in other directions as I matured in academia, but my belief in the power of understanding how impression management operates in classrooms continues.

The following paragraphs summarize some of the basic elements of facework, highlighting components that seem most important for understanding teacher-student interactions. Once these are explicated, I will use examples to illuminate how knowledge of each element might help improve social relations between teachers and students.

- The way people see themselves is defined and negotiated through social interaction. How individuals perceive themselves is affected by how they believe they are being viewed and evaluated by others. Their perceptions of themselves can be improved by successfully creating favorable impressions or deflated by producing an unfavorable set of images. Therefore, everyone is highly motivated to try to manage the impressions others may be forming of them (Goffman, 1959; Hatch, 1994).

- Participants in social interactions take lines of behavior that they anticipate will be accepted as legitimate; but these lines can be called into question by other interactants. When information comes to light that discredits a line taken by an individual, it becomes the responsibility of the person who is "out of line" to explain why the new information does not reflect his or her true self (Goffman, 1967; Hatch, 1994).

- In order to maintain communicative equilibrium, individuals defend their own lines and protect those of their interaction partners. The most basic way to reduce threats to one's face is avoid situations in which these threats are likely to occur. In addition, modesty and hedging are used to protect vulnerable lines from being challenged. When others make small errors that are out of line, interaction partners sometimes ignore these or dismiss them as unimportant, looking the other way to avoid disrupting the social order (Goffman, 1967; Hatch, 1987).

- When acts are egregious enough that they cannot be ignored or played off, Goffman (1967) describes a four-step corrective process for repairing the social order:

> (1) *The challenge*, by which responsibility is taken for calling attention to the misconduct; (2) *The offering*, whereby the offender is given the chance to correct the offence; (3) *The acceptance*, through which the participants signal their acceptance of the offering as a satisfactory means for reestablishing the interactive order; and (4) *The thanks*, through which the forgiven offers a sign of gratitude to his or her forgivers. (Hatch, 1987, p. 102)

Knowing that every individual has a significant stake in how he or she is being perceived by others and that these perceptions are negotiated in social interactions is powerful information for teachers. Creating a favorable impression is in the back of everyone's mind as interactions occur in school. That is true for students and teachers. It is true for primary age students who are just separating from their families; it is true for adolescents who are in the throws of identity formation; and it is true for young adults who are consolidating their perceptions of themselves. It is true for teachers, from novice educators through master teachers. It is true from the first day of school through the end of the academic year.

Understanding that every interaction has the potential to improve or damage every participant's perception of him- or herself can help teachers shape the ways they interact with their students. First, teachers need to realize that how they perceive they are being evaluated by their students has an impact on how they view themselves as teachers, competent adults, and interaction partners. Conversely, teachers need to keep in mind that their students are also projecting and protecting images of themselves as they interact with their teachers, especially when students' peers are witness to the interactions. And it is vital to remember that it is not just what is said (the substantive part of the communication) but what is being projected because of how the exchange is going (the ceremonial part) that counts. It is characteristic of the process that the dynamics of facework interactions between teachers and students go on below the level of conscious awareness. What I am arguing here is that bringing these processes into our consciousness can improve our chances of successfully navigating these important waters.

When individuals adopt particular lines of behavior, they take on some risk if they are not able to maintain those lines when challenges arise. Again, this is true for teachers and students. Teachers have many roles to play in the classroom. Some important roles include instructor, counselor, manager, supporter, and evaluator. In each of these and many more roles, teachers portray themselves in certain ways through what they say and do, and the lines they take in playing these roles will be taken as legitimate by their students or not. In fact, they will be renegotiated every day in the give and take of classroom interaction. Taking lines that they cannot support is risky business. For example, if the teacher qua instructor has presented herself as all knowing and infallible, then when moments arise that reveal stuff she does not know or she makes mistakes while teaching, she will lose face until and unless she can restore her old omniscient/omnipotent line or create a modified version of it.

It is not hard to see the complexity of negotiating the roles of the teacher when some of those roles seem to conflict with each other (Grace, 2012). For example, when teachers take the line of caring supporter, if they are not careful, that role can rub against their desire to be respected as a demanding evaluator. That is not to say performing these two roles simultaneously is impossible (see Chapter 7); it is to say that lines of behavior associated with these roles need to be selected wisely and articulated carefully in word and deed. The same is true for all the lines that make up the many roles of a teacher because events will always arise that will force teachers to defend the faces they are projecting and/or to adjust their lines in reaction to new evidence of their rightful claim to legitimacy in that role.

It is just as important for teachers to remember that their students are also selecting lines of behavior that they think they will be able to sustain in the classroom. They do not want to lose face interacting with the teacher, especially not in front of their peers. Although they will not have an overt awareness of facework principles like I am trying to encourage teachers to develop, they will certainly be taking cues from the teacher and other classroom interactants about enacting the roles they will play.

Everyone in every classroom will be motivated to take lines that can be sustained. A big problem for teachers occurs when lines that give status to some students are established in opposition to lines taken by the teacher. When the teacher's line as a competent classroom manager confronts a student's reputation as a disruptive force, someone's line is at risk of being discredited—so lots of facework will be required to maintain the social order.

Again, teachers need to learn to avoid taking lines that they cannot maintain. Better to include expressions of modesty about one's abilities than to claim infallibility. Better to claim to be doing your best than to expect students to believe you are perfect. Better to acknowledge your errors and play them off as minor missteps than to deny that you have messed up or blame others for your mistakes. This is not the same as coming off as weak or inept; it is about claiming that you are competent but not mistake proof. It is a hard a mountain to climb to be error free all the time, so hedge your bets by acknowledging your humanness.

On the other side of the coin, be prepared to give students a break when they make minor mistakes that bring into question the lines they have staked out in the classroom. If the goal is to maintain the interactive order of the room, then sometimes it is better to look the other way or make light of these screw-ups than to directly confront them and run the risk of creating a win or lose situation. This is similar to advising teachers to pick their battles.

There will be plenty of times when you cannot look the other way. Doing so will call into question the line you have taken as leader of the classroom community; but every out-of-line behavior of every student does not have to be called out every time. You can establish that you are in charge by showing wisdom and patience as opposed to coming off as unforgiving and mean-spirited.

When your students do things that you cannot ignore, giving them room to salvage the faces they have established is vital to maintaining the ritual order of the classroom. Goffman (1967) lays out corrective processes for repairing disruptions in the social order: the challenge, the offering, the acceptance, and the thanks. As we think about these steps, it is important to remember that all communication has a substantive and ceremonial dimension—the overt substance of what we say and the symbolic messages behind what we say and do. Most times, the corrective processes Goffman describes take place at the ceremonial level—that is, they are the subtext of the interactions.

As the teacher, you will most often be responsible for making the challenge when someone's behavior is so far out of line that it cannot be ignored. This is most effectively done by simply describing the misdeed, rather than reacting emotionally or sarcastically or vengefully. You want the problem to be the student's mistake, not your reaction to it. The offering does not have to be a confession of guilt or a promise to never do it again by the student—a return to the expected behavior is sufficient. Your acceptance does not have to be more than returning to the activities of the day; and the thanks might be as subtle as a sigh of relief that the incident has moved out of the spotlight. The big idea to remember here is that no one wants to lose face in conflict-laden interactions, so teachers need to leave some space for students to take responsibility without being humiliated. You want classroom order to be restored, not to escalate the conflict to a place where everyone loses.

It is probably an overly dramatic a story for a book like this, but I had an experience that makes me wish I had known something about facework when I was a 20-year-old soldier stationed in Korea. I was a newly appointed "acting jack" and my radio-teletype squad had just returned to

Camp Casey from 2 weeks in the field. Acting jack meant that I was wearing the stripes of a buck sergeant and had all the responsibilities that went with it, but had not officially been promoted. It was winter in Korea and my men were exhausted from fighting the cold, sleeping in tents, and keeping communications going from remote locations. It was dark when we got back, and everyone wanted to eat, shower, and relax; but we had standing orders that everyone's rifle had to be cleaned and turned in first thing upon returning from the field. When I reminded the squad that they had to clean and turn in their weapons, one man refused, telling me what I could do with myself.

Turns out this soldier was several years older than me, was bigger than me, and had a lot more time in the army than me. I told him that I was giving him a direct order to clean and turn in his rifle. I said I would be back in 20 minutes to see if he had followed orders and if not, I would write him up. When I got back the other soldiers told me that the man I had confronted was out looking for me—that he had loaded his weapon and promised to "kill that acting jack SOB!" The military police came and arrested him before the incident escalated any further.

The next day, a master sergeant who had heard how the incident went down took me aside for a talk that fits well with how Goffman was thinking about saving face in human interactions. My senior colleague told me that cornering the soldier like I did gave him no way to escape except through me. He said I should always give a subordinate a chance to follow orders without being humiliated in the process—to give him or her a way to do the right thing without being shamed in the process. He did not say anything about saving face, but this Viet Nam vet knew a lot about human nature and how to be a leader without being an SOB.

You do not have to be a brilliant social-psychologist to see what was going on in this facework event. I was taking the line of wannabe noncommissioned officer who felt like he had to establish that he was in charge, while my antagonist was trying to save face as an older, more experienced, and more "manly" man. As my mentor tried to explain, it is important to select lines carefully and to be prepared to allow others to salvage lines and save some face rather than create the possibility that one or the other interaction partner will be humiliated. Although set in another context, this is good advice for teachers as well.

Classroom interactions are complex, dynamic, and important. Mega-amounts of substantive communication are passed back and forth throughout the day—that is how school gets done. This chapter is meant to attune new and future teachers to the ceremonial dimension of classroom interaction that makes up the subtext of everything that is said and done as classroom life unfolds—that is how school feels. Understanding that you and your students are projecting faces and taking lines that need

110 J. AMOS HATCH

to be protected during interactions in the classroom can help you establish a positive climate from the start and navigate your way through rough waters should they arise.

To belabor the military comparison one last time, when I went through basic training as one who had volunteered for the draft during height of the Viet Nam war, drill sergeants were there to break you down so that you came to believe that following orders was the only way you could survive. You were not allowed to have a personal face or to take lines of behavior that were opposed to the physical or psychological rigors of basic training. For my money, becoming a drill sergeant with absolute control over every thought and action is the worst model for teachers to adopt. Our goal should be for teachers and students to participate in creating classrooms where everyone has a chance to thrive. Students need strong leaders to ensure that the classroom climate supports everyone's growth. They need competent, caring teachers who communicate substantively and ceremonially that they know what they are doing and are equipped to maintain the order of the classroom. The look in their eyes, the way they orient their bodies, the way they listen, their tone of voice, the things they say and how they say them all send the message that, "I see you as a distinct and valuable human being, and I will do all I can to be sure this classroom operates in a way that can help you be successful here."

REFERENCES

Baiocchi-Wagner, E. (2011). Facing threats: Understanding communication apprehensive instructors' face loss and face restoration in the classroom. *Communication Quarterly, 59*(3), 221–238.

Goffman, E. (1959). *The presentation of self in everyday life*. Doubleday.

Goffman, E. (1963). *Stigma: Notes on the management of spoiled identity*. Simon & Schuster.

Goffman, E. (1967). *Interaction ritual: Essays on face-to-face behavior*. Anchor Books.

Goffman, E. (1971). *Relations in public*. Basic Books.

Grace, G. R. (2012). *Role conflict and the teacher*. Routledge.

Hatch, J. A. (1984). *The social goals of children: A naturalistic study of child-to-child interaction in a kindergarten* [Unpublished doctoral dissertation]. University of Florida, Gainesville.

Hatch, J. A. (1987). Impression management in kindergarten classrooms: An analysis of children's face-work in peer interactions. *Anthropology and Education Quarterly, 18*(2), 100-115.

Hatch, J. A. (1994). Observing and understanding children's social interactions: An impression management perspective. *Dimensions, 23*(1), 21–25.

Payne-Woolridge, R. (2010). Classroom behaviour and facework: Balancing threats and enhancements. *Classroom Discourse, 1*(2), 167–180.

PART IV

**WHAT ARE INSTRUCTIONAL APPROACHES THAT WILL
ENGAGE MY STUDENTS IN SHAPING THEIR OWN
DEVELOPMENT AND LEARNING?**

CHAPTER 13

SCAFFOLDING IS THE MOST POWERFUL TEACHING STRATEGY INVENTED SO FAR

Teachers learn about Lev Vygotsky's (1962, 1978) *zone of proximal development* (ZPD) and *scaffolding* in their teacher preparation programs, but it turns out that the direct application of these powerful ideas does not happen much in real classrooms. Because of the canned curricula and rigid pacing guides that many public school teachers are required to implement, Vygotsky's brilliant model for supporting kids' learning and accelerating their cognitive development is seldom put into practice. It is dismissed as, "nice in theory," but not practical for getting kids through the high expectations that characterize today's schooling.

Turns out, prescribed programs and scripted curricula are not especially effective at doing what they claim (Evans et al., 2010). Even worse, they make it hard for students to experience learning as an engaging, intrinsically rewarding experience. Done poorly, they leave many teachers feeling like low-level technicians and students feeling like objects on an assembly line (Rosenberg, 2011). Trading these ways of organizing and delivering instruction for Vygotskian approaches would improve and strengthen student learning at the same time it invited students and teachers into interactive relationships that make teaching and learning an exciting enterprise for all involved.

Teaching as a Human Activity: Ways to Make Classrooms Joyful and Effective
pp. 113–120

Vygotsky's insight into how learning and development happen is no magic elixir; but it turns out that giving students tasks that are just beyond what they can do on their own and supplying the support they need to accomplish those tasks has the potential to improve the school experience for countless teachers and students. This way of teaching facilitates learning specific content at the same time it builds students' general capacity to learn and accelerates their intellectual development (Bodrova & Leong, 2006). Just as important, kids have a reason to learn because learning becomes a fulfilling human activity that they can get better at. Teachers have an elevated reason to teach because they are directly impacting the improvement of their students' lives—the reason they are in the classroom in the first place.

I have utilized the power of this approach in my own teaching and observed the impact it has had on students and teachers in all kinds of schools. For me, it is not an exaggeration to claim that scaffolding children's learning within their ZPDs is the most powerful teaching strategy invented to date. Even if the constraints of contemporary teaching may limit the possibilities for implementing Vygotsky's ideas into every part of the school day, I believe finding ways to apply them in any part of the day can energize teachers' work and bring joy and fulfillment to the classroom experiences of students.

What follows are two sections: (1) a discussion of four key principles (adapted from Berk & Winsler, 1995) that make scaffolding effective; and (2) a description of ten specific strategies that make scaffolding happen. Included are examples from a variety of content areas at a variety of grade levels. This chapter concludes with an invitation for teachers to use scaffolding to bring more life to their teaching and more meaning to students' learning.

PRINCIPLES OF EFFECTIVE SCAFFOLDING

Scaffolding involves joint effort to accomplish a task that the student can do with support but beyond what the student can do alone. Joint effort means that both you and the student are mutually engaged in working on a task. It is not a task assigned by the teacher and completed by the student. Both work on the task. The message you want to send to the student is, "I know how to do this task and I am going to help you figure it out, too." So, you have to know how to accomplish the task and have the capacity to use language and modeling to support the student's attempts to complete the task. For this model to work, the task has to be beyond what the student can do alone, but within the range of what he or she can do with scaffolding (i.e., within the student's ZPD) (Berk & Winsler, 1995; Bodrova & Leong,

2006). Some tasks are beyond what individual students can do even with expert scaffolding; and these should be saved for later.

Scaffolding relies on the use of language to accomplish a shared understanding of the task between teachers and students. Human learning happens via social interactions between individuals who have certain knowledge, skills and intellectual tools and those who do not (Vygotsky, 1978). The social interactions that distinguish scaffolding from other teaching strategies require teachers and students to participate as partners in coming to an agreement about exactly what the task is that they are jointly trying to accomplish. The success of the student in acquiring the skills associated with the task depends on the pair's accomplishment of a shared understanding of what is expected. This shared understanding happens through the give and take of language. Part of the beauty of the model is that the processes used to reach agreement about the task teach the student how to independently attack similar tasks in the future. The message you want to send here is, "Let's figure out together what we are supposed to do."

Scaffolding takes place best in interactions in which students and teachers feel comfortable and safe. Sometimes the teaching settings in which adults and young people find themselves are characterized by feelings of discomfort and threat. Pressures that often accompany the teaching and learning act lead adults to assume roles such as taskmaster or judge. Some students take the role of victim or even resistor. Effective scaffolding depends on a different kind of teaching and learning environment—one in which both participants are focused on accomplishing the task without the overlay of threats, coercion, or fear of failure. I love this dimension of scaffolding. It turns out that making powerful affective connections with human beings we care about is not just fulfilling everyone's desire for positive interactions, it is good pedagogy! The overriding message behind what teachers say and do during these interactions is, "I believe you can accomplish this task, and I am ready to do all I can to help you."

Scaffolding gradually shifts control over the accomplishment of the task from the teacher to the student. When tasks require completely new ways for children to process information, adults have to provide a great deal of support. Teachers will be doing more talking, more demonstrating, more explaining. They will be thinking out loud in an effort to supply the language children need to master the new thinking processes for themselves. When tasks are not completely new but include some novel elements, good scaffolding means pulling back so that the child contributes more to the solution of the problems at hand. In these cases, you ask more questions and provide more prompts, still scaffolding the areas in which the student needs support, but giving the student increased responsibility for directing the action. The scaffolding process is most powerful when students are gradually given more opportunities to regulate the interactions within the learning event. In fact, handing the management of scaffolding roles and responsibilities from you to your students builds their capacities to *self-regulate* (Berk & Winsler, 1995; Zimmerman, 2002). Students not only learn new content but to monitor and accelerate their learning in all kinds of areas. They are not just learning to think; they are developing metacognition—to think about thinking and to understand themselves as thinkers (Bransford et al., 1999; Pintrich, 2002). As you shift responsibility to students, the message is, "You are a competent learner, and you are figuring out ways to keep track of what and how you learn."

SCAFFOLDING STRATEGIES

I have worked with hundreds of pre- and in-service teachers on improving their skill at providing effective scaffolding. For many, generating strategies on the spot that move a student's learning to the next level seems like common sense. Others rely on more concrete guidance as they learn how to work with students to accomplish tasks the students cannot do on their own. Either way, everyone gets better at scaffolding with practice.

Over the years, I have collected and shared an array of scaffolding strategies that future and current teachers have found useful. Below, I list several of these strategies and give examples of what teachers might say and/or do when they are using these scaffolding moves to support their students' learning. I have tried to include representative knowledge and skills from a variety of subjects and grade levels to demonstrate a range of applications; however, these are just examples. With practice, you will become comfortable generating the right scaffold for the right content at the right moment.

Coconstructing. Coconstructing means overtly completing the activity in cooperation with the student. For example, when a young student is learning to write his name, the teacher places her hand over the student's hand and guides the writing of each letter, naming each letter the two of them are making along the way. Or when a middle schooler is asked to explain how responsibility and decision making are related, the health teacher sits with the student and together they create a chart that lists responsibilities and decision-making events related to personal health practices.

Modeling. With modeling, the teacher goes through the exact processes needed to accomplish the task, showing the student what her or she is expected to do. For example, when a student cannot identify countries that have historically utilized distinct forms of government, the teacher selects a specific country and talks through exactly how she determines if that country fits the criteria for a particular form of government. Or when a young student with special needs is having difficulty counting to 20, the teacher counts out loud with the student as far as the student can go, then continues counting to 20, encouraging the student to join in the counting when she can.

Demonstrating. Demonstrating is modeling with additional explanation. The teacher shows the student how to do the task, while explaining his or her reasoning as the task unfolds. For example, when a math teacher sees a student struggling to solve a linear equation, she goes through each step of the solution, "thinking aloud" as she solves, and explaining why she is doing each step as she does it. Or when a novice violinist is having difficulty with a tricky passage, his instrumental music teacher stops and shows the student the exact fingerings and bowings required for that passage, while explaining the keys to mastering the technique involved.

Directing. Directing means telling the student what he or she needs to do next to move forward with accomplishing the task at hand. For example, when a student seems to be overwhelmed as he tries to solve a physics problem involving acceleration, the teacher tells the him to focus on the elements of the solution one at a time. Or when a student hits the wall during a task requiring her to compare grammatical features of Spanish and English, the teacher has the student review the relevant English structures, then look for comparable grammatical elements in Spanish.

Simplifying. Simplifying means breaking a complex task into smaller parts so that the student can build success one step at a time. For example, when a preschooler is having difficulty matching capital and lower case alphabet letters, the teacher selects a small set of capital and lower case letters that have similar characteristics (e.g., Cc, Oo, Kk, Pp, Ss) as a starting place for building mastery and confidence. Or when an English language learner cannot complete an assignment that requires him to write an essay concerning the causes of World War I, the teacher has him write out a list of causes.

Questioning. Questioning means providing an inquiry that focuses the student's attention on a critical element of the problem to be solved. For example, when a student hits a dead end while trying to complete a task requiring him to classify reptiles and amphibians, the teacher asks, "Can you remember which characteristics of reptiles do not apply to amphibians?" Or when a young reader miscalls a word in text she is reading aloud, the teacher might ask, "Does that sound right?" or "Does that make sense?"

Prompting. Prompting happens when the teacher provides a strategy that will allow the student to move forward with accomplishing the task. For example, when a student finds it difficult to justify her reasoning regarding the main idea of a passage she has just read, the teacher tells the student to go back to key parts of the text and search for evidence to support or refute her thinking. Or when a student cannot make clear connections between geographical features and population patterns, his teacher suggests that he study a map that clearly shows both elements.

Pointing Out. Pointing out happens when the teacher makes direct reference to a critical element in the problem that will help the student be successful at accomplishing the task being addressed. For example, when an emergent reader stumbles while decoding an unfamiliar word, the teacher helps the student see that the initial consonant in the word is the same letter that starts the student's name. Or when a student is stuck trying to figure out what operation to apply to solve a word problem in math, the teacher notes the place in the problem that says, "How many cookies do the children have *all together?*"

Redefining. Redefining means providing the student with alternative words so that he or she can proceed with solving the problem at hand. For example, when a student does not know where to start when asked to identify the nouns in a complex sentence, the teacher paraphrases the instructions, saying, "Let us try to find all the words that name a person, place, or thing." Or when the teacher sees a student struggling to balance a chemical equation, she restates the principles that guide balancing equations and interprets how those principles apply to each step of the problem.

Confirming. Confirming means providing positive substantive feedback so that the student knows he or she is on the right track and can build on that knowledge to complete the task. For example, when a student makes an educated guess about the primary colors needed to make green, the teacher tells the student directly that she is correct, reiterating that, "Yes, we can see that blue and yellow combine to make green." Or when the teacher sees that a student has completed a preliminary step in a geometry proof, he lets the student know that she has successfully accomplished that step (e.g., "Good, you have drawn a figure that shows what needs to be proved").

In real life teaching situations, these strategies blend together, making it hard to distinguish one from the other. Still, it is useful to think about these as separate entities when we are trying to get better at scaffolding our students' learning. As a teacher educator, I had university students role play scaffolding situations with their fellow preservice teachers. I gave the "teachers" in the role-play pairs some real content for a particular grade level, and they had to design appropriate tasks and then supply needed scaffolding moves with a "student" who played at not knowing the content. This is a useful exercise for learning to think about what kinds of scaffolding fit what kinds of content. But, there is no substitute for sitting down with real students who need scaffolding support to move to the next level of understanding or skill development.

Effective scaffolding is embedded in a complex human interaction that includes cognitive, affective, and interpersonal dimensions. It takes practice to effectively establish an ethos of joint activity, use language to accomplish a shared understanding a particular task, nurture a sense of safety and caring, and efficiently shift control of the learning situation to the student. What is great is that teachers get better at implementing scaffolding skills at the same time their students get better at learning specific content and how to become better learners! Both know in their deepest selves that they are sharing something important and fulfilling: learning how to learn. What better gift can teachers give to students they care about and want to succeed?

I do not see the application of Vygotsky's ideas about scaffolding within the ZPD becoming the modus operandi for teaching and learning in the current school climate. The system in place in the schools I know about is set up to push efficient (mostly behaviorist) learning models to the fore. These models are not inherently bad; they have their place for certain kinds of learning in certain situations. But when they dominate all that happens in classrooms, they end up stifling teachers' opportunities exercise their professional judgment and implement pedagogical approaches that stimulate a deeper kind of learning and develop a deeper appreciation for the act of learning itself.

Some teachers connect the discussion of scaffolding to the idea of *teachable moments* that arise spontaneously in the classroom. I like the idea of taking advantage of teachable moments to apply scaffolding strategies to advance students' understanding. It is an important step. But if this is the only scaffolding that gets done, there is too much reliance on the chance that important learning will be addressed spontaneously. It is smarter for teachers to intentionally plan for the creation of teachable moments. This means knowing where students are in their learning; identifying what it is that they next need to accomplish; designing tasks that they can master with support, but not alone; then building in teaching opportunities to scaffold these tasks so that the students are successful.

The unifying idea of this chapter and this book is that teachers are in the profession because they have a steadfast commitment to improving the life chances of the students they teach. I have seen teachers use the scaffolding strategies described above to bring life to classrooms in schools in which the dominant ethos was to prepare students to improve standardized test scores. These teachers worked hard to be sure their students accomplished the achievement goals of the school; but they also intentionally found moments, segments, lessons, sessions, units, (i.e., teaching opportunities) during which they could experience the meaningful learning interactions I am describing here with their students. Like them, you can do more than implement the standard curriculum in the standard ways. You can use strategies like scaffolding to enliven the learning in your classroom and enhance your students' chances of leaving your classroom as happier, smarter, and more confident individuals.

I would love to see the application of Vygotskian principles become the teaching norm in schools; but I am not optimistic that this kind of radical change will happen quickly. However, a quiet revolution, classroom by classroom, in big and small ways, could make life better in schools. It could make life way better for you and the children you teach. It could bring the power of the human heart and mind to the center of the teaching and learning experience. It could change the face of the relationship between you and your students. It could turn the apathy and antagonism that many students express (in subtle and not-so-subtle ways) into the engagement and fulfillment that all humans long for. It could create more opportunities for you to positively impact the lives of the young people you teach. It could help you accomplish your heartfelt goals for becoming a teacher. It could quietly help teaching become an ecstatically meaningful human activity for you and your students.

REFERENCES

Berk, L. E., & Winsler, A. (1995). *Scaffolding children's learning: Vygotsky and early childhood education.* National Association for the Education of Young Children.

Bodrova, E., & Leong, D. J. (2006). *Tools of the mind: The Vygotskian approach to early childhood education.* Pearson.

Bransford, J. D., Brown, A. L., & Cocking, R. R. (1999). *How people learn: Brain, mind, experience, and school.* National Academy Press.

Evans, K. R., Lester, J., & Broemmel, A. D. (2010). Talking back to scripted curricula: A critical performance ethnography with teachers' collective narratives. *Power and Education, 2*(2), 183–196.

Pintrich, P. R. (2002). The role of metacognitive knowledge in learning, teaching, and assessing. *Theory Into Practice, 41*(4), 219–225.

Rosenberg, A. (2011, September 28). An assembly-line education. *Washington Post,* https://www.washingtonpost.com/opinions/an-assembly-line-education/2011/09/26/gIQA8RJR5K_story.html?noredirect=on&utm_term=.4dfc09ddb637

Vygotsky, L. S. (1962). *Thought and language.* MIT Press.

Vygotsky, L. S. (1978). *Mind and society: The development of higher mental processes.* Harvard University Press.

Zimmerman, B. J. (2002). Becoming a self-regulated learner: An overview. *Theory Into Practice, 41* (2), 64–70.

CHAPTER 14

TEACHING STUDENTS TO THINK WOULD ENRICH THE EDUCATION EXPERIENCE AND BETTER PREPARE STUDENTS TO OPERATE IN AN INCREASINGLY COMPLEX WORLD

As someone trained in early childhood education, I taught kindergarten and primary-age students based on tenets based in traditional developmental psychology. Over time, I have come to see much of what I learned and tried to implement as insufficient for getting kids ready for life in the 21st century. My own research, teaching experience and academic study have led me to take long accepted orthodoxies (like Piaget's stage theory of cognitive development) with a grain of salt. Piaget (1964, 1968) basically said that children's thinking capacities are developmentally constrained until they reach the formal operations stage (at about 12 years of age). However, researchers and theorists from disciplines as different as neuroscience, anthropology, and even contemporary developmental psychology (e.g., Bransford et al., 2000; Lave, 1993) have convinced me that some of Piaget's most widely accepted principles do not measure up to what we currently know about how children learn and develop. Bottom

Teaching as a Human Activity: Ways to Make Classrooms Joyful and Effective
pp. 121–131
Copyright © 2021 by Information Age Publishing

line, mainstream education has underestimated children's capacities to think and to learn how to think.

It is clear that students across the pre-K–12 spectrum can learn to think in much more varied and complex ways when teachers provide tasks that require a variety of thinking strategies and support students' attempts to complete those tasks. Further, discoveries about how adults and children learn provide models that I have seen increase children's abilities to think and to intentionally monitor and improve their own thinking processes. Stop and imagine how important that is.

Everyone agrees that the knowledge, skills, and dispositions needed for work life (and all of life) over the next 25 years will be markedly different from what were needed in the past 25. Because of the explosive rate of technological change, we literally do not know what kinds of jobs people will have or what kinds of capacities humans will need to operate in the world. Unless we can help the children who will be working and living in this unknown world to learn to process information and think in complex ways, we will not be preparing them for what lies ahead. It is a big responsibility and a giant opportunity. As teachers, we can start to shift the focus from mastering a set of arbitrary skills to teaching young people to think, to know themselves as capable thinkers, and to revel in the chance to improve their ability to make sound judgments based on their own brain power. What a gift to present to our students and the future of our society!

Knowing what we know about how people learn, teachers can help students learn to think and get better at thinking. In the current climate, schools are often focused on teaching a narrow band of content that is easily measured on standardized tests. The tasks that students complete in school almost never engage their capacities to think. Instead, school tasks focus on low-level information processing that requires mostly memory and skill mastery. Across the curriculum, students are neither metacognitively aware of their own thinking nor taught how to get better at it. This chapter offers some guidance and examples for changing all that.

Thinking and learning to think are hard to assess and get little attention in most schools. The thinking processes and tasks I am suggesting are designed with specific kinds of high-level thinking in mind. There is not room in a chapter like this to cover all the kinds of thinking that should be addressed. I provide a taxonomy of thinking skills (see Table 14.1), descriptions of several important kinds of thinking that teachers at various levels of schooling can address, and examples of how these kinds of thinking can be scaffolded in school.

Curriculum content is included in the examples, but the point is not mastery of the content; the emphasis is on learning to think in different and powerful ways. This approach is about helping kids learn to think in ways that are inherently meaningful, ways that will help them be successful in school, and ways that will support their intellectual development throughout a rapidly evolving future.

As we saw in the last chapter, scaffolding is a powerful tool for advancing students' learning and development in all domains. The kinds of support that Vygotsky described for scaffolding students' learning within their zones of proximal development are precisely what is needed for guiding the development of thinking processes. Vygotsky (1978) taught us that children learn to think by thinking with others. Children learn new intellectual tools by interacting with others who already have those tools. The tasks described below are examples of activities that give children and adults the chance to solve intellectual problems together, building in opportunities for adults to scaffold children's thinking. The tasks are designed with specific kinds of higher level thinking in mind. In Table 14.1, I have organized a taxonomy of thinking skills based on what others have written about thinking processes that children are capable of learning (e.g., Eggan & Kauchak, 2011). This taxonomy provides a framework for teaching kids about thinking.

Table 14.1

Thinking Skills Taxonomy

Information Processing Skills

    Comparing

    Sorting

    Classifying

    Forming concepts

    Generalizing

    Predicting

    Sequencing

    Analyzing relationships

    Considering other points of view

Reasoning Skills

    Inductive reasoning

    Deductive reasoning

    Metaphoric reasoning

    Mathematical reasoning

Creative Thinking Skills

    Brainstorming

    Divergent thinking

    Flexible thinking

Scaffolding is the basic tool adults use to help children build their brain capacity. When adults scaffold children's thinking, they think along with children, making their own thought process evident. They provide explanations, examples, questions, and prompts that model the kind of cognitive processing they want to see in children. Scaffolding is based on the premise that thought and language are intimately connected. Our thoughts are interiorized language; we think in language. Our thoughts are organized in the same form as our spoken and written language. New thoughts enter our brains through language; in fact, they enter our brain *as language* (Berk & Winsler, 1996; Vygotsky, 1962). New ways of thinking do not occur spontaneously in children. In order for children to learn new intellectual skills, they need someone to talk them through how to apply the new language required. When adults are applying Vygotsky's scaffolding strategies to expand children's thinking capacities, they are giving children the language they need to think in new ways.

In the sections that follow, specific thinking skills from my taxonomy are highlighted. I describe the nature and importance of selected ways of thinking, provide specific tasks that teachers can do with students at various levels of schooling, and share examples of the kinds of scaffolding language teachers can use to think aloud with students. The goal is to help kids learn to think, to know the importance of thinking, and to feel energized and empowered because they see themselves as capable thinkers.

As Table 14.1 shows, thinking skills can be divided into three major categories: information processing skills (includes nine specific subtypes); reasoning skills (four subtypes); and creative thinking skills (three subtypes). For the sake of space, I have identified a smaller number to address in detail (classifying and generalizing from the information processing skills category; metaphoric reasoning from reasoning skills; and flexible thinking from creative thinking skills). I try to target different levels of schooling as I describe specific learning tasks, but all the skills in the taxonomy can be taught across the pre-K-12 spectrum, with adaptations for complexity and curriculum content.

INFORMATION PROCESSING SKILLS

Classifying is a cognitive process that involves the use of deductive thinking—that is, reasoning from general categories to specific instances. Once a category of objects or events is identified and named, the task of classifying is to decide if new examples fit (or not) into the category based on the characteristics of objects or events in that category. When working with younger students, teachers start by presenting the child with sets of objects or pictures of familiar items that can be divided into a set that fits into the category you have in mind (e.g., insects) and others that do not fit the category (e.g., other kinds of bugs). The scaffolding needed to model the kind of information processing required for classifying would utilize think-aloud language something like the following:

> I have a bunch of pictures of different kinds of bugs. Some of them are insects and some are not. I am going to look at each picture and decide if it goes in the insect category or not, and say why. This is a picture of an ant. I know that insects have three body parts and six legs. I see that the ant has both three body parts and six legs, so I will put it in the insect category. The next picture is a tarantula. This tarantula has only two body parts and eight legs, so it must not belong in the insect category. What about the bug in this picture? Why do you say that?

Older students can process characteristics of much more complex conceptual categories from a variety of disciplines (e.g., parts of speech, kinds of rock, forms of government, styles of classical music) but the cognitive processing follows the same patterns. Once students can classify objects into single categories, sets of exemplars can be provided that can be divided into two, three, or more distinct but related categories.

The deductive cognitive processing that we are after here is the understanding that categories are formed when objects or events have similar characteristics; and we can decide what objects or events belong in the category by looking closely to see if the characteristics of those objects or events match the category. Scaffolding children's classification attempts should focus on seeing how well the characteristics of the examples fit the characteristics of the category. So, it is important to help children *say why* they classify objects as they do so they can verbalize the mind work needed to do classification.

Generalizing happens when the brain sees patterns of relationship that connect individual observations. When two or more concepts or events can be linked in a patterned way, cognitive constructions that explain those linkages are created. The brain is processing information inductively in order to make general statements about observed events or phenomena. Making valid generalizations gives us the power to explain how different concepts or events are related and to predict how things will happen in the future given the same sets of circumstances. Using an example from geography, we can help students learn to use their brains to form generalizations by providing them with specific instances of how political boundaries are often aligned with rivers, mountain ranges, or other physical features. The content is important and can be taught didactically; but if our goal is also to increase kids' capacities to think inductively, then scaffolding like the following could be used:

I want to figure out if there is something that ties together what we can observe by looking at the boundary lines between some states. I want to be able to say something general by looking at several pieces of specific information regarding state borders. I have some maps that show state lines and topography (physical features of the area). Let us look at the boundary line between Tennessee and North Carolina. First thing I notice is the boundary is not a straight line, unlike the northern and southern borders of Tennessee. The line curves and bends a lot and follows the general path of the Blue Ridge Mountain range. Let's look at a map of the line between Ohio and West Virginia. Again, not a straight line; but this time the boundary follows the route of the Ohio River. One more example is the boundary between Montana and Idaho. Do you see here that the boundary line follows an irregular path along sections of the Bitterroot Mountains, then becomes defined by the Clearwater and Snake Rivers? From these examples, we can say that some state borders, especially those boundaries that are not straight lines, are aligned with natural features like mountain ranges and bodies of water. Let's look at some other state lines to see if they fit this generalization.

The goal for teaching generalizing is to get students to see patterns that connect separate elements. Again, forming generalizations is an essential kind of mental processing that young people can learn how to do and learn how to get better at doing. The world of knowledge includes generalizations from all of the disciplines and subject matter fields, so teaching kids how to recognize and make generalizations is a powerful tool for teaching content as varied as art history, civics, language arts, and mathematics.

Students may need lots of scaffolding early on when learning this kind of information processing, so you should be ready to model your thinking processes by thinking out loud as you explain the reasoning behind your generalizations (as in the example above). As the student takes more responsibility for forming generalizations, he or she may make unsupported guesses about what links phenomena together. When this happens, you should provide more examples and get the student to think with you about why their guesses do not fit the examples given. This mirrors the thinking processes competent adult thinkers use to see if their generalizations are valid or not.

Unlike many school activities, this is not a game of trying to figure out what the teacher says is the right answer. As we saw in the last chapter, scaffolding is an interactive process that can be engaging and exhilarating for young people and their teachers. It is easy for me to get psyched helping kids learn how to think. When I tell students they are learning to think and that is one of the coolest things they could ever learn to do, they know I mean it because I do.

REASONING SKILLS

Metaphoric reasoning happens when people substitute one concept or object for another, making it possible to use comparisons to create symbolic images and reason in unusual ways. Writers, especially poets, use metaphors to generate powerful insights and help readers see things from different angles. When Robert Burns writes, "My love is like a red, red rose," he invites comparisons that involve cognitive processing that includes substituting characteristics of red roses for what we know about love. Young people can start to learn to think inside metaphors when they are guided through the processes of substituting one object or idea for another. Even young children are capable of developing their metaphoric reasoning skills. They are used to using objects symbolically in their socio-dramatic play (e.g., pretending a towel is a superhero cape), so metaphoric reasoning builds on this substitution capacity.

Older students have the chance to apply metaphoric thinking as they interact with high quality literature (both contemporary and classic). You can support the development of this important kind of reasoning at many places in the curriculum, but a logical place to start is to look at how poets use metaphors to bring their works to life. Teaching metaphoric reasoning via a poem like "A Red, Red Rose" might include scaffolding like the following example:

> Sometimes poets use one object to stand for another object or idea. When they want to describe things using words that help readers see those things in different ways, poets sometimes say that they are like other things people know about. Let's look at the first two lines of "A Red, Red Rose" by Robert Burns:
>
> > *O my Luve is like a red, red rose*
> > *That's newly sprung in June.*

Burns is asking us to compare how he feels about his love to a red, red rose. He assumes we know something about newly blossomed red roses that we can apply to our understanding of the depth and quality of his love. If I let my mind think inside the metaphor that Burns is creating, I can imagine that his love is special in a complex, richly textured, natural way. Roses are such fragile and naturally beautiful flowers that they have become a symbol of love itself. They are known to be difficult to grow and need special attention to keep healthy—like love.

There is no good reason to think Burns was being sarcastic when he penned this famous poem, but metaphors like those in "Red, Red Rose" can sometimes have double meanings. If we were cynics, we might turn the symbolism of the red rose on its head and wonder if his love was bound to wither like roses always do. Or we might recall the painful sting of the thorns when we try to get too close to a rosebush. Can you see how powerful metaphors can be for getting your brain to think in different kinds of ways? Tell me what you have to say about the metaphor Burns uses in the next two lines:

> O *my Luve is like the melody*
> *That's sweetly played in tune.*

The emphasis here is on getting young people to concentrate on characteristics of the substitute object or concept and linking them back to the original idea. This involves some tricky cognitive shifting that should be explored in an engaging and open-ended way. We cannot know for sure what authors intend when they ask us to use our metaphoric reasoning, so whatever we personally think is perfectly fine. What we are after here is to develop the brain's capacity to think metaphorically, so being able to explain *why* we make the interpretations we do is critical.

As in the example, once students become comfortable thinking of ways elements of comparison objects fit the original constructs, they can be guided to think about ways the comparison object does not fit the apparent intent of the metaphor (e.g., roses have thorns and do not last very long). This secondary analysis can be especially useful in teaching young people how to use their brains to think inside metaphors. Younger students of course will need more scaffolding (especially modeling, suggesting, and questioning) to get better at thinking metaphorically; but students of all ages can learn that their brains are powerful tools that can be used to reason in a variety of ways.

CREATIVE THINKING SKILLS

Flexible Thinking is brainwork that allows individuals to think in unusual ways. Parents and teachers almost always ask children to complete tasks that have a predetermined outcome and to answer questions that have predetermined answers. Young people get too few opportunities to use the parts of their brains that are capable of thinking creatively about a variety of ways to accomplish tasks or answer questions. The point here is that children can learn to be more flexible in their thinking when given the chance (and it is our job to give them the chance).

The starting place is for students to be able to learn make distinctions between convergent and divergent thinking—and to see the essential nature of each. The answers to some questions require factual responses, so it makes sense that different people would come up with the same solutions (i.e., their answers would converge). However, there are lots of questions to which there are multiple, equally appropriate responses, so it becomes possible, even desirable, for a variety solutions to be generated (i.e., answers would diverge).

One kind of activity that facilitates the development of flexible thinking involves creating imaginary situations and asking open-ended questions that encourage children to think differently about those situations. When the situations are made up, young people are invited to utilize their creative imaginations without being constrained by the expectation of converging on the "right answer." As in the example below, asking the right kinds of open-ended questions signal children that novel responses are desirable:

> I want to use my brain to practice thinking about what I would do if I were in a make-believe situation. I am going to imagine I am a giant living in a world where everyone else is the size of my thumb. Here are some questions that could help me think about what it would be like in that imaginary world: What would be the best things about being a giant? What would be the worst? How could I make friends with the little people around me? What could I do to help my little friends? What would I need to be careful about in this imaginary place?
>
> I think the best thing about being a giant would be that nobody could tell me what to do. I would be bigger than anyone else, so I could do whatever I wanted and go wherever I wanted. The worst thing is everyone would be afraid of me, and I would have no friends my own size. I could try to make friends by being nice to everyone and getting down on the ground so that I was closer to the little people. I could help the little people in lots of ways. I could easily move things that were too heavy for them to move; I could lift them up so they could see for a long way; and I could help them stay safe if they had any enemies. I would have to be careful not to sit or step on my little friends, and I would have to speak softly so they were not scared by my loud voice.

In this example designed for use with younger students, the adult did all the talking. It would be unusual, even when introducing this kind of flexible thinking activity, for the child not to begin contributing ideas right away. Remember that in scaffolding, the adult only provides the level of support needed to advance the child to the next level in his or her zone of proximal development. So, if the child understands the context and the aim of generating unusual solutions, then the adult can step back and provide prompts and feedback.

Activities like this teach young people what flexible thinking feels like and show them that they can do it. Such activities give students the chance to imagine themselves in a pretend situation, then think creatively about how to respond. The make-believe quality of the scenario will set the stage for children to get away from the feeling that there is one correct answer that the adult knows and the child is trying to guess.

Older children can practice flexible thinking by generating unusual solutions to real world problems that are related to the aims of the school curriculum. It is easy to think of complex issues the world faces that are appropriate content for social studies or science, producing questions like: What are some ways we could address the deep political divisions in our country? Or, what are some possible solutions to the climate crisis? The key here is to keep the focus on encouraging flexible thinking, so questions need to be those that encourage the generation of many possible solutions, not finding the one best answer.

In sum, students love to explore the agility of their brains. I can feel differences inside my head when I shift from one kind of brainwork to another. The brain works differently when I am listing all the state capitals I can name than it does when I am listing all the unusual uses I can think of for a laundry basket. I spend time setting up activities so students can feel the shifts in their brains and learn to recognize how amazing their capacities to think really are.

We know that even young children can learn to think and to think about their own thinking (Bransford et. al., 2000). It is important as we implement activities like those described above that we are intentional about helping students use their metacognitive capacities to become more aware of themselves as able thinkers and to see themselves getting better at thinking. They can learn the lessons of the official curriculum at the same time they are learning how to think in ways that are underemphasized in most school settings. Best of all, they can learn to see thinking as the most powerful attribute a human can possess and to celebrate how good they are at exercising that defining human quality. It is hard to imagine a more important gift from teacher to student.

REFERENCES

Berk, L. E., & Winsler, A. (1995). *Scaffolding children's learning: Vygotsky and early childhood education.* National Association for the Education of Young Children.

Bransford, J. D., Brown, A. L., & Cocking, R. R. (Eds.). (2000). *How people learn: Brain, mind, experience, and school.* National Academy Press.

Eggan, P. D., & Kauchak, D. P. (2011). *Strategies and models for teachers: Teaching content and thinking skills.* Pearson.

Lave, J. (1993). The practice of learning. In S. Chaiklin & J. Lave (Eds.), *Understanding practice* (pp. 3–32). Cambridge University Press.

Piaget, J. (1964). Development and learning. In R. E. Ripple, & V. N. Rockcastle, *Piaget rediscovered: A report of the conference on cognitive studies and curriculum development* (pp. 7–20). Cornell University School of Education.

Piaget, J. (1968). *Six psychological studies*. Random House.

Vygotsky, L. S. (1962). *Thought and language*. MIT Press.

Vygotsky, L. S. (1978). *Mind in society: The development of higher psychological processes*. Harvard University Press.

CHAPTER 15

IN ORDER TO OPERATE SUCCESSFULLY IN THE 21ST CENTURY, STUDENTS NEED TO BECOME CRITICALLY LITERATE CONSUMERS OF INFORMATION IN ITS MULTIPLE FORMS

Traditional forms of literacy instruction still have a place in schools; students must learn to effectively read, write, speak and listen. But, the information age and technologies that generate new forms of "text" dominate the real-life literacy experiences of our students. In order to prepare students to operate in a future that is already upon us, we have to go beyond teaching literacy the way it has been done for decades. Students need exposure to approaches that develop critically literate consumers of all kinds of written and graphic forms of communication. They need critical literacy skills that are readily applied to the analysis of all the forms of communication they are exposed to every day. They need to learn insights and develop dispositions that will enable them to adapt to communication technologies we can only imagine today. This chapter provides concrete examples of classroom approaches that give students the

Teaching as a Human Activity: Ways to Make Classrooms Joyful and Effective
pp. 133–143
Copyright © 2021 by Information Age Publishing

tools needed to analyze the complexity of postmodern communication through a critical eye.

I have been around for a pretty long time. The small southern Utah town in which I spent the first 9 years of my life did not get TV until just before my family moved from Cedar City to Salt Lake. I listened to basketball games, boxing matches, classic comedy shows, and Saturday night dramas on the radio (mainly at my grandmother's house). I remember the first time I saw color TV was at a girlfriend's house when I was a young teen. I wrote my first 20 or so articles on legal pads and paid a typist to put them into manuscripts that could be snail-mailed in triplicate to journal editors. My first computer was supplied by Ohio State University, when I went to work as an assistant professor at its Marion campus. I kept my flip-phone for way too long, and I am just now getting used to having Alexa at my beck and call. I have seen an amazing array of technological changes in my lifetime.

Like many in my generation, I marvel at what new technologies can do *for* us at the same time I worry about what they may be doing *to* us. In fact, one of those early hand-written articles was entitled: "Technology and the Devaluation of Human Processes" (Hatch, 1984). But, I do not count myself as a Luddite. I want to acknowledge up front that my goal in this chapter is to accept and respect the perspectives and experiences that most readers of this book will bring to their reading. Most of you are "digital natives" (Hamilton & Edge, 2016, p. 320) who have grown up in the technological age and see the burgeoning advances that surround us as essential, inevitable, and even natural. Given that these changes in large measure define how humans communicate (in the here and now and who knows about the future?), I am arguing that we need to do a better job in school of helping children and young people learn how to operate in the digital age.

I think young kids still need to learn how to read and write. I support calls for expanding how we think about literacy, but learning how to get meaning from and put meaning into traditional text seems essential. Trouble is many literacy programs remain too heavily focused on the *traditional text* part, so students are not really being prepared to process communication forms that dominate their daily experiences (Marsh, 2005). I am not ready to sunset efforts to teach kids the skills necessary to read and write effectively; I am ready to broaden definitions of literacy and to help young people become more savvy consumers of information in its many forms.

MULTIPLE LITERACIES

For the purposes of this chapter, I will use the term *multiple literacies* as a counterpoint to the traditional school emphasis on teaching kids to read and write. Multiple literacy can be simply defined as the "ability to communicate effectively and absorb information through a variety of mediums" (Bales, 2019, p. 1). This way of conceptualizing literacy recognizes that today's world offers many ways to send and receive information. Bales (2019) identifies four modes that should have a prominent place in school curriculum: visual, digital, technological and textual literacy. While these categories sometimes overlap and may not directly address all forms of communication available now or in the future, they offer an organizer for thinking about literacy more broadly and provide a platform for discussing ways alternative literacy capabilities might be developed in the classroom.

Visual literacy is "an individual's ability to understand and evaluate information presented through images such as pictures, photographs, symbols, and videos" (Bales, 2019, p. 1). The key word here is "images." Much of the information conveyed via the media that inundates our students is image-based, as opposed to text-based. So, people are getting input from television, smart phones, computers, video games, virtual reality devices, and other technologies that are made up mostly of images. In order to effectively process this image-based information, students need to develop visual literacy skills that go beyond simply looking at images; they need to learn how to assess "the message the image is trying to convey or the feelings it is designed to evoke" (Bales, 2019, p. 3). For starters, they need to develop an awareness that those who create the images have some purpose in mind and that images are selected, designed, and/or altered in order to accomplish that purpose. Students can learn to critique visual information in the same ways they examine the accuracy, quality, and reliability of text. Activities like the following give a flavor for what instruction in visual literacy might include.

Elementary-aged children can work together to analyze sets of images that are designed to sell various products. They can search through paper or online ads, looking to answer questions like: "What are the advertisers trying to sell?" "Who are they trying to get to buy their product or service?" "What are they showing to try to get people to buy their product?" "What are they not showing that might make you think twice about buying their product?" Students can also create their own ads, locating or creating images that would portray strong selling points for a particular product for a particular audience.

Middle schoolers can learn to look for and explore the meaning of visual symbols that appear in print and electronic media. An engaging way to attune students to the use of visual symbols would be to have them search the internet for flags of nations that include interesting symbols and to find out what those symbols stand for and why they were included in the flags' designs. This could be followed up with a design contest, in which individuals or groups create a school or community flag with symbols that reflect what they want to be represented.

High school students can study the pictures, illustrations, and photos included in their history textbooks. For example, in the section of American History that covers the Civil War, students could examine the images included and ask questions such as: "Why did the authors choose this photograph?" "What do you think about when you see this illustration?" "How does this image make you feel?" "Do you think everyone feels the same way when they see this picture?" "What images were left out when this section was put together?" Similar kinds of activities could be utilized to analyze video or movie-length representations of historical events.

Some scholars and researchers worry that the graphic forms that are replacing text-based information are directly influencing how brains (especially developing brains) work when humans process incoming stimuli (e.g., Gottschalk, 2019; Postman, 1985). I am not sure of the implications (good and bad) of that hypothesis, but I am sure that the technology-infused world we live in (and our students will inherit) will be dominated by image-based information. Given the pervasiveness of images across all forms of modern technology, it seems imperative that we support the development of children's visual literacy in school.

Digital literacy has been defined by the American Library Association as "the ability to use information and communication technologies to find, evaluate, create, and communicate information, requiring both cognitive and technical skills" (2013, p. 2). I like this definition because it includes the last phrase: "requiring both cognitive and technical skills." My observations and experience tell me that even students who are adept at the technical skills part are not always up to speed on the cognitive part. They are very good at clicking their way around the internet, but not so good at interpreting and making valid judgments about what comes up on their screens. So (per the American Library Association definition), they can *find* information, but may not know how to *evaluate* it. Further, seems to me that they get too little opportunity to utilize digital formats to *create and communicate information*. Sample activities that get at some of what seems to be missing are suggested below.

Younger students may need more support with the technical skills part of digital literacy than older kids, but the cognitive dimension needs to be addressed as well. Many elementary students will be familiar with computers, smart phones, and the internet; but not all. Some will know about accessing the vast amount of information available electronically; but not all. So attention must be paid to doing all we can to put our students, no matter their age, on an even playing field with regard to access and understanding. For sure, even early grades students need to learn how to find information and to evaluate the information they find.

Upper elementary and middle school students can participate in activities that require them to search for information from a variety of sources and compare the quality and usefulness of what is found. For example, they might be assigned to search for different perspectives on income inequality and to look closely at the sources that come up and analyze the evidence opposing sides use to make their cases. They could be asked to create a graphic representation of their findings and conclusions, utilizing cutting-edge presentation software.

High school students can go more deeply into learning to be critical of the glut of information available via websites, blogs, social media posts, and many more electronic sources. With support, they can learn to fact check questionable content and use reliable sites to track misinformation and outright lies back to their original sources. They can be taught to always ask, "Who stands to gain from altering images, twisting the truth, or promoting fabricated stories?" Like their younger counterparts, they too can practice using the latest software to organize and communicate the information they have analyzed.

Technological literacy is "the ability of an individual, working independently and with others, to responsibly, appropriately and effectively use technology tools to access, manage, integrate, evaluate, create and communicate information" (Montgomery Schools, 2016, p. 1). There is not much to distinguish this definition from that of digital literacy above, so the discussion of how to improve students' technological literacy will be focused on what sets this literacy dimension apart from the others.

What seems different is the emphasis on using technology "responsibly," "appropriately," and Bales (2019, p. 3) would add, "ethically." We are talking about interacting with various technologies (e.g., social media, online video sites, text messaging, video games, artificial intelligence, virtual and augmented reality) in ways that protect the user and respect the privacy and human rights of others. Just being able to navigate the complex cyber world that is so readily available to students does not mean that they know how to do so safely, legally, and respectfully. We do not have to come across as preachy to provide experiences that help students see the potential pitfalls that can befall any unwary tech user.

Elementary students can be introduced to the concepts of responsibility, appropriateness, and ethics as general themes that have direct implications for utilizing technology. Adjusted for their maturity level, these general concepts can be taught didactically then applied to situations involving technology. For example, younger students can learn that maintaining freedom means taking responsibility—that having the opportunity to access the internet means making responsible decisions about what will be accessed and what will be shared. Tied to responsibility, they can develop an understanding of what is appropriate and what is not—examples of appropriate and inappropriate uses of technology can be contrasted and discussed. Elementary students can learn that ethical behavior includes treating others as you would like to be treated—examining and discussing ways that technology must not be used to harm individuals, communities, and cultures.

Middle school students will have a broadening knowledge and experience base and be able to make more direct connections among responsibility, appropriateness and ethics within a variety of technologies. Protecting the privacy of yourself and others needs to be stressed as an essential responsibility—this can be done via descriptions of ways that privacy can be compromised and examples of potential outcomes when it is. Appropriateness includes understanding that technology makes possible access to material that is not suitable for young people—these concerns can be explored from legal, moral, and safety perspectives. The ethics of cyber-bullying should also be an important topic for this age group—with an exposition of how devastating such practices can be, embedded in discussions of the negative consequences of bullying in general.

High school students can become more proactive in developing their technological literacy. They can study and form arguments to support their position on issues such as net neutrality—exploring the responsibilities of users and giant technology firms. They can debate the relative appropriateness of other countries' efforts to influence US elections via cyber attacks on candidates they do not favor—this can include an exploration of if this is done, how it is done, and how effective it can be. Older students can also explore the ethics of data mining that pervades the practices of the major companies that dominate the tech world—taking on such questions as, "Who owns the data?" "Should these people have unlimited access to our information?" "Should they be able to sell information about us to whomever will pay?" Across the age span, students who are technologically literate need to understand not only how to operate digital devices, but to do so safely, responsibly, ethically, and thoughtfully.

Textual literacy most closely parallels traditional notions of literacy. It has been defined in terms like the following: "Literacy is the ability, confidence and willingness to engage with language to acquire, construct and communicate meaning in all aspects of daily living" (Alberta Education, 2016, p. 1). At a basic level, textual literacy refers to a person's ability to assimilate information through reading and to communicate effectively in writing. However, I agree with Bales (2019) that textual literacy also includes the ability to "analyze, interpret, and evaluate" (p. 2) what is being read and written. I am going to assume that if you are reading this, you have been (or soon will be) prepared to teach young kids to read and write and/or to advance the reading and writing development of older students. Given that assumption, I will forgo including examples here and make a bridge to the second major theme of this chapter, which directly addresses the "analyze, interpret, and evaluate" elements just mentioned. As I focus on critical literacy, I will be suggesting exemplary classroom applications that get at textual literacy and the other literacy forms along the way.

CRITICAL LITERACY

Serafini (2003) describes *critical literacy* as "an approach that addresses the social, historical, and political systems that affect literacy and what it means to be a literate person in contemporary society" (p. 7). Rooted in the pioneering work of emancipatory educator, Paolo Freire (1970/2005), critical literacy is about raising consciousness regarding relationships among language, power, and culture. This approach to literacy instruction helps readers think of language as a social construction through which social ends are accomplished. Teachers invite students to critique the status quo as represented in most of the text they encounter and to participate in addressing injustice and inequality in their reading, writing, and being in the world. As Meller (2008) summarizes, "As students learn about the relationships among themselves, language, texts, and the world, they develop the potential to initiate social change" (p. 30).

What I want to emphasize in this section is the power of applying a critical lens to processing information, no matter what form that information takes. Critical literacy provides insights and tools that can help students analyze communication in all its forms. The principles of critical literacy can be applied during the teaching of all the literacy types in the previous section: visual, digital, technological and textual. Reading with a critical eye means asking questions of what is being presented, no matter the platform. For critiquing traditional text, Reisboard (2013) suggests questions like: "Who wrote this text? What does the author want me to believe? What information was included or excluded during the writing of this text?" (p. 469). It is easy to modify questions like these to fit digital, visual and technologically mediated communication. We just need to broaden our conceptions of "author" and "text."

It seems all the more important to be critical consumers of information given the dramatic technological changes happening around us. As we have seen, individuals, institutions and even governments have taken advantage of technologically-based media to manipulate the truth, create absurd conspiracy theories, and divide us as a people. As teachers, we do not have to stake out a political position to help our students become more prudent consumers of information, and the principles of critical literacy give us guidance into how we can do that.

Most of what I know about critical literacy and how to apply it in class-rooms I learned from doctoral students in literacy education at the University of Tennessee. That is one of the joys of being a professor at a research-intensive university—you get be on the committees of super smart, dedicated professionals who are studying something in great depth. I was lucky enough to work with one such professional, Wendy Meller, while she completed her coursework and a dissertation focused on critical literacy (2008). Wendy was also a graduate teaching assistant in our Urban-Multicultural Teacher Education Program, so I got to see her teach what she was learning to future teachers. As a result of our shared experiences, Wendy and I were able to collaborate on some articles and book chapters linked to critical literacy (e.g., Hatch & Meller, 2009; Meller et al., 2009; Meller & Hatch, 2008), and many of the ideas in this section come from those experiences. As above, I will briefly describe some activities teachers at various grade levels can use to develop critical literacy skills and dispositions in their students, being sure to include activities that address the multiple literacies focus of this chapter.

A major focus of Wendy's dissertation study was using read-alouds with critical literacy literature in primary classrooms (Meller, 2008). This is an excellent technique for introducing elementary-age students to critical literacy, one that builds on the common practice of reading aloud to students. Collaborating with Danielle Richardson, a teacher who applies a critical literacy approach in her urban classroom, Wendy and I (Meller et al., 2009) described the steps for planning and implementing read-alouds using critical literacy literature as follows:

- *Select a book* that is a representation of high quality children's literature and that allows for discussion of social issues of interest and importance to the students, remembering that "texts are not critical in and of themselves; it is the conversations that take place around the text that qualify as critical" (p. 77).
- *Preview the book* by looking for places that might spark conversations about critical issues as well as identifying key words that might be unfamiliar to students so these can be introduced in a prereading activity.
- *Develop critical questions* that can be used to initiate discussions as the read-aloud unfolds, writing these on sticky notes and pasting them at appropriate places in the book.
- *Conduct a minilesson* that activates students' prior knowledge, making connections to previous learning and to their experiences related to the social issues raised in the book.

- *Do a picture walk,* taking the students through the illustrations in the book and having them make predictions about the story, characters, and setting.
- *Read the story,* stopping to ask the questions on the sticky notes and encouraging discussion, concluding with questions like: "Who is telling the story?" "Why do you think the author wrote this story?" "How is the story the same and different from experiences you have had?" "What can we do to make things better?"

Of course, a similar set of procedures could be applied to lessons that help children critically analyze "text" in electronic formats. For example, animation companies produce videos and movies that include lots of opportunities for making connections to children's lived experiences and the inequities that characterize many dimensions of society. Even young elementary students can learn that producers of electronic media take a particular perspective, that they have a particular audience in mind, and that there are always alternative ways of thinking about their messages. Watching these kinds of media does not just have to be a Friday afternoon "reward" for having a good week; learning to critique them can provide a powerful tool for developing students' critical literacy across technological platforms.

Middle school students can learn to be critical as they navigate their way through a world of ever evolving technological advancement. We can help raise their consciousness about how what is communicated and how it is packaged can influence their lives. As one example, students could be assigned to analyze the form and content of popular video games, answering questions such as: "Who are the marketers of this game trying to reach?" "What devices are being used to attract players?" "How are different cultural groups represented? "What are the underlying messages in this game?" "How does the content of this game square with real life?"

A central tenet of a critical literacy approach is that once critical consciousness is raised, students should have opportunities and the disposition to take action to initiate social change (Meller, 2008). High school students can develop critical analytic skills by examining evidence of social injustice that is embedded in images that are used to portray marginalized groups. These images are included in print media like newspapers, magazines, and books as well as all kinds of electronic formats. A sample assignment that includes an action element might have students search for images of Native Americans (or any cultural group) across print and digital formats, collect these images using some kind of electronic program, complete an analysis that includes an examination of if and how stereotypes play a role in why these images were included and what they were intended to portray, create a presentation that summarizes the find-

ings from the analysis, and distribute the presentation to appropriate outlets.

In summary, kids still need to be adept at reading and writing, but they
need instruction and experiences that enable them to process and generate information in forms other than traditional text. As teachers, we need
to lead our students to become critical consumers of information, no matter how it is packaged. We need to give our students tools for operating
safely, intelligently, and ethically in the information age, the technological
age, and whatever unforeseeable age they are bound to encounter over
the next decades. Expanding our vision to include a multiple literacy perspective and taking seriously the advantages of teaching critical literacy
will give us a foundation for providing students with cognitive and technological skills necessary for operating in a rapidly changing world.

REFERENCES

Alberta Education. (2016, February 19). *What is literacy: Literacy definition, components and elements of the progressions.* Alberta Ministry of Education, https://edu-
cation.alberta.ca/literacy-and-numeracy/literacy/everyone/what-is-literacy/

American Library Association Digital Literacy Task Force. (2013). *ALA Task Force
releases digital literacy recommendations.* http://www.ala.org/news/press-releases/
2013/06/ala-task-force-releases-digital-literacy-recommendations

Bales, K. (2019, July 3). *Multiple literacies: Definition, types, and classroom strategies.*
ThoughtCo. https://www.thoughtco.com/multiple-literacies-types-classroom-
strategies-4177323

Freire, P. (2005). *Pedagogy of the oppressed* (30th anniversary ed.). Continuum.
(Original work published 1970).

Gottschalk, F. (2019, January 31). *Impacts of technology use on children: Exploring the
literature on the brain, cognition and well-being.* Directorate for Education and
Skills, Organisation for Economic Co-operation and Development. https://
www.oecd.org/officialdocuments/publicdisplaydocumentpdf/?cote=EDU/
WKP%282019%293&docLanguage=En

Hamilton, C. E., & Edge, E. (2016). Emerging role of technology to support early
childhood pedagogy. In L. J. Couse & S. L. Recchia (Eds.), *Handbook of early
childhood teacher education* (pp. 319–332). Routledge.

Hatch, J. A. (1984). Technology and the devaluation of human processes. *Educational Forum, 48*, 243–252.

Hatch, J. A., & Meller, W. B. (2009). Becoming critical in an urban elementary
teacher education program. In S. L. Groenke & J. A. Hatch (Eds.), *Critical pedagogy and teacher education in the neoliberal era: Small openings* (pp. 219–232).
Springer.

Marsh, J. (2005). Digikids: Young children, popular culture, and media. In N. Yel-
land (Ed.), *Critical issues in early childhood education* (pp. 181–196). Open University Press.

Meller, W. (2008). *A critical literacy case study: The journey from pre-service exploration to in-service implementation* [Unpublished doctoral dissertation]. University of Tennessee, Knoxville.

Meller, W. B., & Hatch, J. A. (2008). Introductory critical literacy practices for urban pre-service teachers. *The New Educator, 4*, 330–348.

Meller, W. B., Richardson, D., & Hatch, J. A. (2009). Using read-alouds with critical literacy literature in K–3 classrooms. *Young Children, 64*, 76–78.

Montgomery Schools. (2016). *Technology literacy definition.* Maryland Technology Literacy Consortium. https://www.montgomeryschoolsmd.org/departments/techlit/

Postman, N. (1985). *Amusing ourselves to death: Public discourse in the age of show business.* Penguin.

Reisboard, D. (2013). Going beyond the efferent: Teachers' critical literacy development using picture books. *Journal of Modern Education Review, 3*(6), 468–477.

Serafini, F. (2003). Informing our practice: Modernist, transactional, and critical perspectives on children's literature and reading instruction. *Reading Online, 6.* http://www.readingonline.org/articles/art_index.asp?HREF=serafini/index.html

CHAPTER 16

TEACHERS NEED TO UNDERSTAND AND DEMONSTRATE TO THEIR STUDENTS THAT TECHNOLOGY HAS VALUE IN SO FAR AS IT ENHANCES THE HUMAN EXPERIENCE IN SCHOOL AND BEYOND

If you are reading this book front to back, you may be surprised because the thesis of this chapter seems to contradict the emphasis on teaching technological literacy in the preceding chapter. It feels awkward to me too. However, my view is that children and young people must learn to operate intelligently and ethically in a high-tech world (hence the focus on multiple literacies from a critical perspective in Chapter 15), while they should also become more savvy about how technological advance has the potential to diminish our humanity or at least alter the experience of being human in ways that are not all good. This chapter is about recognizing some of those potential threats to our humanness and finding ways to address those threats. The chapter offers examples of ways technology can be harnessed to enhance human learning and development in the classroom.

Teaching as a Human Activity: Ways to Make Classrooms Joyful and Effective
pp. 145–152

Giant technology companies, tech gurus, and the media have convinced us that technology has unquestionable value and that technological advance is automatically positive. Hardware and software that were originally designed to enhance human capacities have taken on a life of their own, and now it is virtually (pun intended) unthinkable to challenge the primacy of technological advance. In school, teachers have the opportunity to turn the current paradigm on its head and use many amazing forms of technology to enhance the human experience. Any technology utilized in school settings should have as its purpose to improve students' chances of learning important content, developing important skills, and becoming more fully human. Teachers and students need to see technological advances as providing opportunities for learning and growth, not just the next cool thing.

As in the last chapter, I want to aver that I am not a Luddite. I am not automatically against technological progress and certainly do not want to return to a mythical time when things were simpler and better. What I am after is a view of technology that insists that it be managed to suit human purposes, as opposed to technological advance being its own driving force and to hell with what that means for being human. As mentioned in Chapter 15, I worried in the 1980s that a phenomenon I named "technological inflation" (Hatch, 1984, p. 244) was systematically threatening the development of human processes in school and society. My hypothesis from almost 40 years ago has proven correct. In that original article, I argued that,

> Technological advancement compounds itself, generating more technology and often ignoring the human elements it was originally designed to serve; that as technology is layered upon itself, we become insulated from the basic human processes and, as a result, alienated from ourselves; and that education ... is deeply involved in the inflation of technological impact and in the systematic devaluation of human processes. (Hatch, 1984, p. 243)

The examples used in the 1984 article seem pretty passé when I read them now, but the logic of the argument stands and is much more easily supported today. Technological inflation happens when the purposes of invention and innovation shift from serving some useful human purpose to generating new systems and products because progress demands it or because tech companies have convinced us that we must have the latest version of what they are selling. Instead of using technology to solve human problems, the focus is on improving or replacing existing technologies. As we become more engaged with (even dependent on) the latest innovations, we are in danger of losing track of the very processes that make us human.

By way of example, I will point out a few obvious technological "advances" that I believe have served to insulate us from the human processes identified in Chapter 8 (i.e., perceiving, knowing, loving, patterning, decision making, creating, valuing, and communicating):

- The act of *perceiving* the world via our senses is dramatically altered when mediated via technologies associated with virtual or augmented reality.
- The need for *knowing* a lot about a little or a little about a lot has been diminished because of access to information available with a click or two on the internet.
- *Loving*, finding love, and expressing love have increasingly shifted from being face-to-face experiences to ones that take place on line.
- The need to develop intellectual capacities related to *patterning* is being replaced by algorithms that make cognitive connections and uncover complex relationships for us (often without our knowledge or permission).
- *Decision making* that has been dependent on human judgment is being replaced by developments in super computing that make possible the direct application of big data to everyday problems.
- The act of *creating* is being modified by the application of computer assisted programs across the arts, humanities and sciences.
- *Valuing*, which was once considered to be impossible for machines to accomplish, is currently being programmed into the technologies associated with artificial intelligence.
- *Communicating* is likely the human process that has been most dramatically impacted because of technologies that mediate talking and listening, for example e-mail, cell phones, texting, and all the social media platforms.

Again, all I am trying to do is to get you to think about how technological advancements (no matter how cool, intriguing, or powerful) might have the downside of reducing our chances and our students' chances of becoming more fully human. I get that some see a kind of post-human future as inevitable, and they are just fine with that; but I see the loss as too steep a price for mindlessly adding more and more layers of technology between ourselves and our humanity. But it is not an all or nothing deal—we can help our students see that technology has usefulness because it gives us the chance of experience and *develop* our humanness at the same time we caution them about the pitfalls of letting technology *redefine* our humanness.

The movement of our species toward becoming post-human beings has long been a popular theme of science fiction writers and futurists; but science fiction has turned into science fact and the future has turned into now. Yuval Harari (2017) sees post-humans as the merger of humans, computers, algorithms, and biochemical devices. For me, this brings up popular media images of cyborgs (cybernetic organisms) that have both organic and biomechanical body parts. The post-human world is upon us. Think of all the advancements in technology that enhance the capacities of medical practitioners to diagnose, treat, and operate; and consider the evolving use of robotics, computers, and biomechanics to make artificial limbs that are controlled by the user's brain—and these are just examples of what is possible right now in one field.

Harari agrees with me about the potential dangers to our humanness of the explosion of technology. In an article in which he was interviewed about his book, *Homo Deus: A Brief History of Tomorrow*, Harari (2017) used the example of people using increasingly sophisticated biometric sensors to monitor what they do and how their bodies react to show how such technologies can impact our sense of humanness. In his words,

> The most important invention that is spreading now is biometric sensors. They may become ubiquitous. Humans will consult their biometric data to determine how to live. That is really interesting and scary stuff, because we will no longer be in charge of our identity. We will outsource our executive decisions to biometric readings of our neurochemical signals to decide how to live. (Thompson, 2017, p. 5)

The development of artificial intelligence (AI) is another technological advance that many believe poses a serious threat to the human species as we know it. Reminiscent of science fiction thrillers in which robots go rogue and take over from their human masters, serious scholars, scientists, and philosophers worry that artificial intelligence could create a world in which, "Human beings will exist largely for the machines, rather than being served by them" (Kotkin, 2020, p. 145). Wakefield (2017) says it even more starkly: "Bees exist to pollinate flowers, and maybe humans are here to build machines" (as cited in Kotkin, 2020, p. 145).

The point is that technical advances like these, which have obvious benefits, also carry significant risks. When we become dependent on technologies like these (and others we can barely imagine), we lose something of ourselves, of our identities, of our humanness. When technology development is fueled by purposes other than enhancing our innate humanity, we can blindly slip into a post-human existence in which all of our experiences are mediated by forces outside our intellects, outside our hearts, outside our souls. When technological inflation is left to run rampant, we will continue to be insulated from our humanness by layer upon layer of technological innovation.

Rohit Bhargava has been tracking what he calls, "non-obvious mega-trends" for over a decade. In his latest book, Bhargava (2020) identifies and describes what he has discovered to be the ten most a salient trends that impact how we work, think, and act today. As you would expect, the list includes mostly outcomes related to technological advance, such as "instant knowledge" (we have immediate access to information—threatening the need for mastery or wisdom), "data abundance" (big tech companies are mining data about us as we use their products—and selling the data for profit), and "protective tech" (smart devices can monitor our lifestyles and predict outcomes—taking over for personal responsibility and endangering our privacy).

But, what I found most interesting among the 10 was a megatrend Bhargava called "human mode." Based on his analyses, he asserts that, "In a world booming with technology, there are signs that our humanity matters more than ever before (Bhargava, 2020, p. 114). He notes that human beings need to belong, and they yearn for "interactions with real people who are compassionate and skilled" (p. 113). I resonate with what he is saying; and I think that others are experiencing a new kind of anomie because of technologies that insulate us from meaningful human connections, causing us to feel isolated and alienated. As citizens and teachers, it is our responsibility to take heed and react.

Below are some things we can do in school to utilize technology to enhance, rather than diminish, human connections and capacities. I will describe three interconnected general approaches: (1) Raising consciousness about the byproducts of technological change; (2) Modeling the application of technology to enhance humanity; and (3) Nurturing human connections. As in previous chapters, I will include example lessons for students at different educational levels.

Raising consciousness about the byproducts of technological change means providing activities that help students recognize the powerful but mostly invisible effects technological innovations can have on their experience of being human. Elementary students can do comparative studies of how human activities have changed over the centuries as a result of technological innovation. Early grades can study progress in elemental areas such as transportation and communication. Older students can complete studies of more specialized areas such as medicine and manufacturing. Students can create time lines that show gradual progress in the past compared with the rapidity of change we see today. Part of the point of these studies should be that human needs have been met in different ways across time, and that while the progress made in these areas has been dramatic and beneficial, potential downsides have also emerged as these technologies have proliferated.

Middle school students can trace the histories of the tech devices they use today, looking back at how these devices have evolved and exploring how advances in the devices have impacted their users. For example, a study of smart phones could work backwards from looking at what these devices can do today, to what has been recently added, to early versions of cell phones, to landline phones, to the invention of the telephone. Careful attention should be paid to examining the original purposes for telephones and exploring how those purposes have changed as technology has advanced. Students can create presentations in which they identify the positives and critique the possible downsides of smart phone technology (e.g., health risks, distracted driving, fear of missing out, loss of privacy, etc.).

High school students can complete a critical examination of the purposes and consequences of using everyday technology. For example, they could engage in a careful study of social media platforms, comparing what each site offers and what purposes they claim to serve. Students could critically analyze what the websites purport to be their purposes, comparing what the platforms say to what the students' know from using or hearing about how others use the social media being studied. Students can be assigned to pro and con teams and prepare to debate reasons why certain social media sites are good or bad for individuals and society. While they must stay "in role" during the debate, time should be given after the debate to discuss students' real thinking about the topic.

Modeling the application of technology to enhance humanity means walking the talk by demonstrating that technology can have a positive impact on the human experience if it is applied in ways that improve human capacities and serve human needs. The modeling I am talking about here includes teachers' explanations for how they are using particular technologies to enhance particular human ends and why they are eschewing the use of other technological options. In elementary classrooms, this might include carefully selecting the games that are provided for students to practice math skills, apply science content, or explore social studies concepts, emphasizing that electronic games can be fun and engaging at the same time they advance kids' knowledge and skills (as opposed to being packed with sexualized characters and gratuitous violence).

Middle schoolers can be shown that the vast array of information available on the internet can be culled for sources that make possible an improved experience of being human (as opposed to insulating ourselves from our humanity). For example, teachers can utilize historically significant documentaries to help students see how certain groups have been exploited, marginalized and debased by other groups, opening the door for the development of understanding, compassion, and human decency.

High school students can be given assignments in which they are required to utilize high tech tools to accomplish human purposes (as opposed to just using them because they are available). For example, they could be given the task of using their cell phones and presentation technology to create a self portrait that includes photos, videos, images, audio, and text that provides insights into what makes them unique (e.g., their families, friends, communities, histories, experiences, avocations, strengths, aspirations). Portraits could be projected in class and/or posted on a secure internet site.

Nurturing human connections means emphasizing the value of having experiences that are uniquely human, creating space in the school day for children and young people to express, enjoy, and enhance their humanness. The point here is to build in activities that recognize and celebrate what it means to be human. This way of thinking parallels the major theme of this book (especially the human processes explored in Chapter 8). Some specific examples that offer alternatives to commonly used technology-meditated activities are included below.

Elementary students who have fallen behind and been identified for extra services (usually based on the response to intervention model) can receive the support they need directly from the teacher, rather than via the computer programs that are widely used across the United States. While these programs might help some students needing a boost and a few who are seriously struggling, most of these programs turn out to be ways to meet the letter of response to intervention expectations, but do little to meet the needs of students who require support. My view is that good teaching means knowing what kids can do and what they need to learn to do better. With or without response to intervention, good teachers find ways to send the message to their students that, "I am here to do whatever I can to make sure you learn as much as you can." That might mean including time with computer programs for reinforcing some skills; but face-to-face time during which one human connects with another cannot be replaced.

Middle school students can experience learning activities that require them to cooperate directly with their peers to complete some meaningful task. These activities need to be more than just "group work." They need to follow principles of cooperative learning that have been shown to help students learn important content at the same time they develop an appreciation for working in concert with others—principles like heterogeneous grouping, teaching collaborative skills, group autonomy, maximum peer interactions, equal opportunity to participate, individual accountability, positive interdependence, and cooperation as a value (Jacobs et al.,

2002). Taking time to build cooperative effort into school activities gives students opportunities to develop human attributes at the same time they explore subject matter in engaging ways.

High school students can be given assignments that require them to make direct contact with other human beings outside of class. One example would be to have students work in groups to identify an issue that is salient in their home community, explore possible solutions, and take action to address the issue. Key here is for students to find out what those who live in the community are thinking. That means talking directly with those people and keeping a careful record of what issues, solutions, and actions community members think are salient. Electronic media may be useful in such a project (e.g., for recording interviews or taking photographs), but it is the direct human contact that makes such projects especially valuable.

If you are leaving this chapter with the sense that I think technological progress is inherently bad, I have failed. I just do not want to perpetuate the feeling that it is inherently good. There is no doubt that our students will be living in a world in which technology will have an increasingly important role. This is a book about preserving the humanity of teaching, so finding ways to understand and try to manage the potentially negative consequences of emerging technologies seems important for us and for our students.

REFERENCES

Bhargava, R. (2020). *Non-obvious megatrends: How to see what others miss and predict the future*. Ideapress.

Harari, Y. N. (2017). *Homo deus: A brief history of tomorrow*. HarperCollins.

Hatch, J. A. (1984). Technology and the devaluation of human processes. *Educational Forum, 48*, 243–252.

Jacobs, G. M., Power, M. A., & Loh, W. I. (2002). *The teacher's sourcebook for cooperative learning: Practical techniques, basic principles, and frequently asked questions*. Corwin Press.

Kotkin, J. (2020). *The coming of neofeudalism: Warning to the middle class*. Encounter Books.

Thompson, D. (2017, January 20). The post-human world: A conversation about the end of work, individualism, and the human species with the historian Yuval Harari. *The Atlantic*. https://www.theatlantic.com/business/archive/2017/02/the-post-human-world/517206/

Wakefield, J. (2017, February 22). Tomorrow's cities: Nightmare vision of the future. *British Broadcasting System*. https://www.bbc.com/news/technology-37384152

PART V

**WHAT CAN I DO TO ENSURE
MY SUCCESSFUL INITIATION
INTO THE TEACHING PROFESSION
AND AVOID BURNOUT IN THE FUTURE?**

CHAPTER 17

TEACHERS NEED TO DESIGN AND MONITOR THEIR OWN SOCIALIZATION INTO THE FIELD

All individuals go through a process of socialization when they enter new social contexts, including the contexts in which they work. Teachers have to learn the subtexts of the settings in which they work, including the unwritten expectations for getting along. The transition from student to teacher roles is a key socialization step, and it can be especially difficult because of the oft opposing expectations associated with each role. This chapter describes powerful socialization processes at work in school settings and gives specific advice for monitoring and taking action to be sure teachers are practicing socialization "by design," rather than "by default."

My socialization into the teaching profession was 100% by default. I fell right into the value system of my college of education at the University of Utah. Based on what my professors taught me, I never questioned that my first responsibility as a teacher would be to help my students maximize their potential and become self-fulfilled. When I began my career, I was so in love with being a teacher that I could not believe they were paying me to show up each day. I was so into the kids I was teaching in Kansas City, Missouri that I never stepped back and thought about the contrasts between the "child-centered" approach I had learned in college and the "behaviorist" program I was implementing in Kansas City. I was so

Teaching as a Human Activity: Ways to Make Classrooms Joyful and Effective
pp. 155–163

thrilled to be doing what I thought was important work that I never considered how I was being shaped by the expectations, mores, and unwritten rules that were at play in my urban school system, my all-Black elementary school, and the behavior analysis program I was hired to deliver.

Same deal when I moved to a different context in Jacksonville, Florida—I was so engrossed with being a teacher, I did not reflect on the powerful socialization processes that were going on inside and around me. It was not until I started studying sociology in graduate school that I was awakened to the reality that as humans, we are driven to fit in, to belong, to not stick out in social settings. When we enter new social settings, our first concern is to appear as if we belong there. In order to do that, we have to psych out what is considered to be appropriate behavior—what we are supposed to say and not say, do and not do. Some of this is written down, but most of this knowledge is tacitly understood by those who are insiders in a particular social context.

We have all felt the unease of entering an unfamiliar social setting—think the first day at a new church or showing up at a family reunion of your new or prospective in-laws. Starting a new job is especially stressful because so much is riding on your demonstrating that you fit in. Starting a teaching career can be super anxiety-producing because you have spent 16 or more years in the "child-student" role, with someone else telling you what to do, when, and how. Then you are expected to take on the opposite, "adult-teacher" role, where you make the decisions and tell others what to do (Hatch, 1984, p. 61).

Learning about how socialization works and reflecting on my own initiation into teaching led me to try to help other new teachers do a better job of recognizing, monitoring, and shaping their own socialization into the field. Based on some basic sociological principles I learned from influential scholars like Howard Becker (1970) and my mentor, Rodman Webb (1981), I published a piece in the 1980s with the subtitle: "Socialization by Default or by Design" (Hatch, 1984). Those principles have held up over the years, and I have worked with hundreds of future educators to help them understand and manage the difficult transition from student to teacher.

Socialization can be defined as "the process through which individuals learn and internalize cultural norms, codes, and values. This process enables entry into and sustained membership in one or more social groups" (Saras & Perez-Felkner, 2018, p. 1). In my original article, I relied on Becker's (1970) general construct of "socialization by default," pointing out that socialization into the teaching profession (as in other social contexts) takes place below the level of consciousness; that is, individuals who are new to the teacher role "do not consciously make choices among alternative behaviors, but internalize the expectations of the role without overt awareness of the process" (Hatch, 1984, p. 62). As I argued back then and have preached over the course of my teacher education career, teachers can have a hand in our own socialization by becoming aware of and giving direction to the process (i.e., practicing "socialization by design"). Being aware just means bringing the thoughts and feelings we experience as we are trying on our new roles into our active consciousness.

I had a valued colleague at the University of Tennessee who was expert at guiding our students through their yearlong internship experience. One of her favorite exhortations to these preservice teachers was, "Fake it till you make it!" I understood what she meant, but I had to add, "It is okay to fake it so long as you are aware that you are faking it." Webb (1981) describes what I take to mean faking the teacher role without being conscious that you are doing so:

> Commitment grows through a series of seemingly innocent acts, each one of which brings individuals deeper into their official role. At first, they awk-wardly do the things expected of them and experience considerable role distance in the process. They are self-consciously aware that they do not believe their own acts and are not committed to them. Their behavior does not reflect their inner feelings. But as time goes on, these acts become less foreign. Individuals begin to have a bigger stake in carrying them off convincingly, until, without being aware of it, they begin to believe their own propaganda. They become committed to their roles *not by choice but by default*. (p. 244, emphasis added)

Being aware is a necessary but not sufficient counter to socialization by default. Teaching is difficult work and the environment in schools is much more complex than most work settings. That makes learning the ins and outs of teaching and the figuring out the unwritten rules of working in schools pretty intense. Those difficulties are compounded because education is not great at inducting new members into the field. Other fields provide a prolonged, stepwise entry into the world of professional practice, what sociologists call "anticipatory socialization" (Shepherd, 2015). Not so much for the field of education. In our business, we usually provide a relatively brief "student teaching" experience, during which future teachers have limited chances to take on the full teacher role; then once hired, novice teachers are expected to assume the same responsibilities as a seasoned educator from their first day on the job. In Moir's (2003) words, new teachers "find themselves doing two jobs at once: being a teacher and learning to teach" (p. 1). It is hard to step back and reflect on the processes of socialization when you are in the midst of experiencing them. It is even harder to react to the powerful forces involved when you are feeling overwhelmed with trying show that you are up to challenges of being a new teacher.

I know how difficult monitoring and managing the socialization process can be. I have experienced, observed, and systematically studied teacher socialization. I mentioned above that my own induction into the profession was socialization by default—I was simply oblivious to the forces that were shaping what I thought, said, and did. In our urban-multicultural teacher education program at the University of Tennessee, we were lucky because ours was a 5-year program. A small faculty worked intensively with a cohort of 20–30 preservice teachers for a year and a half, including a yearlong internship. I think we did a much better job of anticipatory socialization than most programs; but many of the smart, savvy, and well-prepared new teachers we sent out still told us they had difficulty managing their socialization into the field.

Trying to understand the difficulties our graduates reported back to us led me to design a study that followed a cohort of students from entry into our program through the first 2 years of their teaching careers. Most of the data from the study consisted of qualitative interviews, during which I asked the participants to describe their perspectives on teaching, the roles of the teacher, and the impact of their experiences on how they felt and thought about students, teaching, and schools. I wrote up some of the findings from this project in articles that described how they thought about teaching in urban contexts while they were preservice teachers (Hatch, 2007, 2008); but I never reported findings directly related to their socialization into the real world of teaching.

I collected and analyzed my data from their first 2 years of teaching, but I did not publish those findings because I was afraid the data excerpts (quotes from the participants) I would have to use to make the case would caste the good people who agreed to work with me on this project in a negative light. These were my colleagues and friends, and they trusted me with their honest descriptions of what they were experiencing as new teachers. I could not in good conscience use their words to show that they had great difficulty managing their own socialization into teaching. What this experience showed me is the power of teaching contexts (in different kinds of schools in different parts of the country) to impact socialization into the field. I did not want to appear to "blame the victims" by using my former students' words to demonstrate the power I am talking about.

I have some of the same feelings about what I am about to say concerning the values and norms I have seen enacted in many schools over the years. I am not trying to bash teachers or tar the field with broad generalizations that characterize *all* educators or schools. I am trying to give readers a heads-up about some of the attitudes and behaviors they may encounter as they enter the profession—attitudes and behaviors I hope they will not internalize as a result of *socialization by default*. Being forewarned does not diminish the power of these kinds of unspoken norms and values, but it does give new teachers a chance to be alert to what is going on and the opportunity to resist being co-opted without realizing it.

In some schools, the teacher break room or lunch room can become a place for what amounts to gossiping about students and their families. We advised our field rotation students and interns to stay away from such settings if possible, and to refrain from participating in the negative talk when they could not avoid being there. We explained that they had a professional obligation to hold confidential any sensitive information they learned about children and families. But in the spirit of anticipatory socialization, we also encouraged the future teachers in our program to stay close to their mentor teachers and learn all they could about the real world of teaching by experiencing what real teachers do in the classroom and out. Do you see the rub? If it is the norm for your mentor to hang out in the teachers' lounge where sensitive information or titillating rumors are openly shared, what is an intern or student teacher supposed to do?

So, imagine the extra pressure to conform if you are a newly hired teacher and find out that similar unprofessional conversations are "normal" in your school. You may be able to simply avoid being in such spaces (I always ate lunch with my elementary students for this and other reasons); but you will be trying to fit in, so avoiding places where teachers hang out may seem to work against being accepted as a colleague. Unless you are a very strong person, it is unlikely that you will openly challenge your new colleagues. I have talked with teachers who have made it their goal to change the tenor of these conversations by offering positive insights about what was working in their classrooms (as opposed to joining in on the negative banter). As a new teacher, you may not be able to do much at first, but you can remain acutely aware of the discomfort you feel while witnessing such gossip sessions and resolve to not to get caught up in the destructive ethos of these settings and start participating.

A related refrain that reflects the value system of teachers in some schools is, "These kids just cannot learn." This usually applies to certain groups of students and is sometimes part of the school's climate even when nobody says it out loud. It is a pretty good tip-off that someone is labeling them as less than normal when Black children, poor children, children whose first language is not English, or special education students are referred to as "These kids" or "Those kids." It hurts my heart when I hear young human beings talked about as if they were a nuisance that gets in the way of teachers having a good day. I am astonished to think that teachers would want to continue in the classroom if they think their students are hopeless cases. What in the world do they think their job is, if not to help children and young people be successful?

The image I tried to create for my preservice teacher education students was to picture the seasoned teachers who expressed or demonstrated this "cannot learn" attitude sitting in a college classroom when they were preparing to be teachers. I asked my students to consider what these now jaded teachers would be thinking and feeling when they were at the beginning phases of their career. After we agreed that they probably started with the same ideals and aspirations as the current students, we wondered together what happened to bring about such a dramatic and disappointing change. The students brainstormed ways to not let themselves turn into teachers they did not want to become. Being aware of the powerful potential of being socialized by default was always a big part of the takeaway from these discussions.

Another trope that makes the hair on the back of my neck stand up is, "These parents just do not care." Same deal: "These parents" always refers to some identifiable group or community that is assumed to be deficient. It is hard for me to imagine the thought process that would lead to this blanket conclusion. It must reveal some kind of not-so-hidden bias against people who come from different backgrounds, social strata, cultures or races. Parents from every ethnic group and every walk of life love their children and care about their children's education. Some parents may be so overwhelmed with holding things together, or feel so alienated from schooling, or are so intimidated by the system that they do not behave the ways that teachers expect; but that does not mean they do not care.

I sometimes wonder what my K–12 teachers thought of my family. When the six of us moved to Salt Lake, my mom emptied bedpans and mopped floors at the LDS Hospital, but my dad could not hold a job because of a debilitating seizure condition. We were scraping bottom financially, psychologically, and socially. Seeing how I came to school (on days I did not skip), my teachers lectured me on brushing my teeth and scrubbing my neck; they coached me on washing out my own clothing; and they sent social services to our apartment to check on the wellbeing of my siblings and myself. My parents loved their kids as much as any parents anywhere, but they were overwhelmed with the stresses of trying to survive from one day to the next. My parents valued education and wanted us to succeed in school; but they were never actively involved at school in the same way as other parents. They assumed it was the school's job to take care of school stuff, they felt awkward and inferior talking with education professionals, and they just did not have the time or energy to be engaged. Too many other parents are in similar circumstances.

When I hear teachers say, "Those parents just do not care," I cringe. I cannot help but think that it must be some way to rationalize why the teachers are unable to be effective in reaching their students. Teaching is tough. Reaching every student may be impossible. But why are you there if not to do everything you can to reach every child you can each time you get the chance? There is great joy in making a difference in the lives of our students. There is great satisfaction in taking responsibility for doing our best to do what we know is right. We can guide our own socialization so that we internalize and operationalize commitments that elevate us as teachers and people (as opposed to looking for someone else to put down or something else to blame).

As a final example of the kind of negative ethic that can be a part of the belief system of some schools and teachers, I want to talk about the idea of writing off some students as not worth our time and effort. This can be part of a general ethos that new teachers need to be aware of so they do not get socialized into believing it; but, what makes it even more danger-ous is that it has been institutionalized in many places when students identified as "bubble kids" get more attention and instruction, at the expense of students the system does not think have a chance of succeed-ing.

All of this is tied to the test-based accountability regime that drives schooling today (Hatch, 2015). Schools are under great pressure to improve standardized test performance, and this pressure is passed on to teachers, who need to show progress on their students' scores from year to year. In many schools, especially those serving students who have diffi-culty scoring well on the tests, a kind of educational triage takes place.

Since getting as many kids as possible to a certain level of proficiency is rewarded by the testing system, schools identify "bubble kids" who are close to but not at that level. These students get extra instructional time and attention because they provide the best chance for the school to show measurable improvement. It is assumed that the "high" kids will be fine with less time and attention; but the big losers are the children and young people who are below the bubble category. These students are essentially written off—like the mortally wounded in a war zone field hospital who are moved to the back of the triage line because they are unlikely to make it anyway.

To me, this is as close to educational malpractice as anything I know about; yet it is standard practice and even policy in many schools (Booher-Jennings, 2005; Graue & Johnson, 2011). I get it that schools and teachers are under tremendous pressure to improve test scores—I take the whole accountability-based-on-standardized-testing regime to be a deeply flawed way to assess the effectiveness of schooling (Hatch, 2015). But, as a teacher responsible for doing everything in your power to improve the life chances of your students, I do not see how you can sleep at night if you reduce the educational opportunities of any child for the sake of moving a number on a spreadsheet at the end of the year.

The plea here is simple. Even if you are "told" to identify and provide extra help for bubble kids does not mean that you have to accept that it is right to do so. You can meet the expectations of the system without internalizing the warped values behind some of them. Even if it is an unwritten way to game the testing system that all the other teachers do, that does not mean that you have to "go along to get along." You can work hard to maximize *every* child's chances for success and at the same time maintain your professional integrity.

These examples may seem dramatic, but they are real. As your career unfolds, you will develop and refine your own ethos as it relates to teaching, students, parents, and schooling. You can be self-consciously aware of how your values evolve, or you can uncritically internalize the mindsets of those around you. You can adopt the attitude that these forces are much bigger than you, or you can resolve to do all you can to hold onto the dreams that led you to the important work of shaping young people's lives. You can capitulate to the processes that lead to socialization by default, or you can do your best to mindfully monitor your socialization by design.

When my university students talked about ways to keep from becoming the jaded teachers they sometimes saw in the schools, they always talked about finding others with whom they could find community and support. They talked about being careful to seek out workplaces where their value systems as new teachers matched the ethos of potential schools. But, knowing that they might not have unlimited job choices, they saw the need to connect with others in and out of their schools and in and out of the profession, so they would not be isolated as they negotiated their way through the transition from student to teacher (see Chapter 19). Invariably, they committed to staying in close contact with the other members of their teacher prep cohort—and they have.

Our program also emphasized the importance of reflective journaling to help students learn to monitor their reactions to what they were experiencing. Many former students have told us that keeping a journal was invaluable in helping them step back from the pervasive influence of the immediate experience of being a new teacher and reflect on how they were thinking and feeling about how they were being impacted by the forces around them. If you are like me, the act of organizing thoughts and feelings into written words, forces you to consider things differently than when they are just passing through your mind. So, keeping a journal that keeps track of your socialization can help you reflect on and make sense on your initiation into teaching.

Other ideas that our preservice teachers recommended to each other for managing their own socialization included making sure that they keep learning through workshops, taking classes, and personal reading; taking time away from teaching to renew, refresh, and stay healthy; and scheduling a regular (e. g., monthly) self-check, when you stop to evaluate how you are seeing your progress toward achieving your goals for yourself as a teacher. In order to monitor and shape your own socialization, you need to start with a firm answer to the question: "What kind of teacher do I want to be?" For me, an inexorably linked question is: "What kind of human being do I want to be?" Your answers to these questions provide a beacon to guide you and a baseline for assessing how well you are doing. Everyone has a different way of handling the challenges of being a new teacher; but no matter their differences, everyone has the opportunity and responsibility to be reflective about what is needed to be the teacher and person they want to be.

REFERENCES

Becker, H. (1970). *Sociological work: Method and substance*. Aldine.

Booher-Jennings, J. (2005). Below the bubble: "Educational triage" and the Texas accountability system. *American Educational Research Journal, 42*(2), 231–268.

Graue, E., & Johnson, E. (2011). Reclaiming assessment through accountability that is "just right." *Teachers College Record, 113*(8), 1827–1862).

Hatch, J. A. (1984). Student to teacher transition: Socialization by default or by design. *Teacher Education and Practice, 1*(2), 60–64.

Hatch, J. A. (2007). Pre-service teachers' beliefs about urban contexts. *Journal of Urban Learning, Teaching, and Research, 3*, 25–36.

Hatch, J. A. (2008). Preservice teachers' perspectives on critical pedagogy for urban teaching: Yet another brick in the wall? *Teacher Education and Practice, 21*, 128–145.

Hatch, J. A. (2015). *Reclaiming the teaching profession: Transforming the dialogue on public education*. Rowman & Littlefield.

Moir, E. (2003). *Launching the next generation of teachers through quality induction*. National Commission on Teaching & America's Future.

Saras, E. D., & Perez-Felkner, L. (2018, August 28). Sociological perspectives on socialization. *Oxford Bibliographies*, https://www.oxfordbibliographies.com/view/document/obo-9780199756384/obo-9780199756384-0155.xml

Shepherd, G. (2015, October 26). Anticipatory socialization. *Wiley Online*. https://onlinelibrary.wiley.com/doi/abs/10.1002/9781405165518.wbeoss195

Webb, R. B. (1981). *Schooling and society*. Macmillan.

CHAPTER 18

IT IS RISKY FOR TEACHERS TO DEPEND ON STUDENTS' LOVE AS THEIR MAJOR SOURCE OF INTRINSIC JOB SATISFACTION

Teachers almost always say that they are in the profession for the intrinsic rewards associated with working with children and touching the future—not for the (below average) pay or (non-competitive) job benefits that are the extrinsic rewards of teaching. Healthy human relations between teachers and students are vital to classrooms where the kind of rich learning that we are talking about in this book goes on. But, too many teachers are disappointed and burn out because they put too much emphasis on having their students love them as the basis for their job satisfaction. As examples in the chapter will show, deep kinds of reciprocal caring are often created in classrooms where humans interact in meaningful, consequential ways; but in this complex relationship, depending on students' love to keep you going will often lead to poor decision making and disillusionment.

The case I want to make here is not that the extrinsic rewards of teaching are adequate for motivating those who work directly with children and young people. What U.S. teachers are paid is an embarrassment when compared to other countries of similar size and resources (Organisation for Economic Co-operation and Development, 2015). Further, teacher pay over the course of a career ranks among the lowest when compared

Teaching as a Human Activity: Ways to Make Classrooms Joyful and Effective
pp. 165–172
Copyright © 2021 by Information Age Publishing

with occupations requiring similar academic preparation (Will, 2018). Even worse for me, U.S. teachers have far less autonomy and enjoy much lower relative social status than their counterparts around the globe (Strauss, 2018). So, it seems pretty self-evident that extrinsic motivation will not be sufficient to attract and keep the committed and competent teachers we so desperately need. It is the intrinsic rewards of our profession that make us want to teach and want to stay in the classroom. I think the intrinsic rewards of teaching are many. Examples are spread throughout the chapters of this book, and I will highlight some of these positives below; but first I want to wave a potential red flag: Teachers who depend on receiving love from their students are cruising for a fall.

Across the hundreds of written applications I have read and interviews I have conducted with students seeking admission into our teacher education program at the University of Tennessee, probably the most common response to the "Why do you want to teach?" question was: "I love children." I counted that as a good answer, but always looked for elaboration or asked follow-up questions to see if the candidates were thinking carefully about what loving children meant to them. We always tried to give folks who were vying for the limited number of spots in our program the benefit of the doubt (some years we took less than 50% of applicants); but sometimes it was clear from some interviewee responses that "I love children" meant something close to, "I need the love of children."

I strongly believe that some people have an affinity for working with children and young people. I think I am one of those people. Even as a preteen, I recall organizing activities for the younger children at family reunions and other gatherings. As I described in Chapter 9, I did not plan to make a career of teaching until I had an epiphanic moment during a visit to a Head Start classroom as part of a course experience at the University of Utah. My decision to change my major and career plans had a lot to do with love. I loved the idea of touching the lives of children. I loved the idea of shaping the future. I loved the idea of having a career that made a difference. I still do. But, even though I thrived on the human connections I made with my students, I never expected love or depended on receiving love from my students as a source of job satisfaction.

For me, it is the "expected love" or "depended on receiving love" part that makes all the difference. Teaching provides the opportunity to share lots of time and lots of unique experiences with young human beings. When teachers and their students are deeply engaged in important work that everyone cares about, strong emotional connections are bound to develop. The feelings associated with those connections are among the most powerful intrinsic reward or our profession. The red flag I am trying to raise is meant to signal that it is possible for teachers to put themselves in an impossible situation when they distort the feeling of shared engagement in ways that make them dependent on receiving affection from their students. When this kind of dependence develops, the judgments, decision making, and actions required of a professional teacher can be jeopardized.

Thinking about a parallel phenomenon experienced by some parents may help make my point. Many of us have observed parents who are so worried about alienating their children that they are afraid to establish firm boundaries, provide consistent discipline, or ever just say, "no." They come off as wanting to be friends with their offspring, rather than being responsible adults. Often called "permissive" parents, these individuals create an atmosphere that puts the child in charge of the parent, which can lead to unfortunate outcomes for both. In Lloyd's (2016) words, "Children can end up feeling entitled to getting what they want, not what they need: the self-restraint, patience, and other character traits that will help them succeed in life" (p. 1). Same problem for teachers and students. When teachers are unwilling to be the adult in charge, the consequences are not good for them or their students.

To be clear, I am not recommending that new teachers fall back on the old saw: "Don't smile 'til Christmas!" You do not have to be an ogre to be a responsible teacher (or parent). I am just warning that some of the same needs, desires, and personal inadequacies that lead parents to avoid responsible parenting can impact teachers' abilities to make professional decisions in the classroom. Teachers who live for the love of their students are setting a trap from which it will be hard to escape. Like the spoiled offspring of permissive parents, students will learn quickly that they are in charge, and they will manipulate their teachers' emotions in order to get their own way.

Applying a more dramatic example related to parenting, there is evidence that some teen pregnancies occur when the young mothers want babies because they want someone to love them unconditionally (Planned Parenthood, 2010). Still children themselves, they do not feel loved by the adults in their lives, so they seek to fill their own emotional needs by having a baby. Of course, this is wrong on so many levels; but the same kind of transference is possible for some teachers entering the classroom. As I mentioned, we sometimes denied entry into our teacher education program because we were worried that some applicants *needed* the love of children. This was always a tough call, but sometimes it was clear that the candidate did not possess the emotional maturity to be successful in the classroom.

Another tip-off that we observed in written applications and interviews was when prospective teachers announced that they were more comfortable being around young people than adults. On its face, that is a problem because so much of the work of teaching takes place in interactions with other adults (e.g., coworkers, community members, administrators, and parents). But, at a deeper level, it is troublesome because it portends the possibility of an unhealthy relationship between themselves and their students. I remember a woman I almost dated in Jacksonville who accused me of teaching elementary students because I could not be successful in adult relationships. She was doing her best to hurt me because I was ending our relationship. I never let her insult get to me; but you can see the point: It is possible to conceive of teachers who depend on the attention and affection of young people because they lack opportunities to fulfill those needs outside of school. Bottom line, you cannot be a successful teacher unless you are capable of being an adult and willing act like one.

Teaching is complex work. It requires practitioners to wear many hats, some of which seem to be contradictory. Most occupations require workers to enact roles that sometimes conflict with other roles that are built into their jobs. For sure, teachers confront several role conflicts. Some of the contrasting role sets that teachers have to negotiate include: encourager versus evaluator; facilitator versus instructor; nurturer versus disciplinarian; emancipator versus monitor; mentor versus supervisor (Hatch, 1999). These conflicts are difficult enough; we do not want to add "friend versus teacher" to the list.

When teachers' sources of motivation depend on receiving the affection of their students—when they get caught trying to fulfill the role of friend—they are going to find great difficulty balancing expectations built into the teaching role. Describing the treacherous nature of the inherent conflict between the "friendly" versus the "teacherly" role, Woods (1987) noted that, "overindulgence in friendship can mean that it is difficult to break free when the situation demands one to be teacherly. This in turn can undermine the basis of the friendship" (p. 123). So, trying to be friends with your students is a lose-lose situation. You will neither be an effective teacher nor a genuine friend.

Linsin (2011) makes a compelling case for the risks associated with expecting to establish friendships with students in a post entitled: "Why You Should Never, Ever Be Friends With Students." He lists seven reasons why it is a bad idea:

- They will not respect you;
- They will stop listening to you;
- They will challenge you;
- Rules will no longer apply;
- Consequences are taken personally;

- Accountability no longer works;
- You become lax in following your classroom management plan (pp. 1–2).

On a practical level, these warnings make perfect sense to me. Just as with permissive parenting, when teachers are unwilling to draw boundaries and exert their role as the one in charge, students will take every opportunity to manipulate classroom situations to their advantage. This makes life miserable for teachers and unproductive for students. Children and young people do not want a faux-peer who wants to appear to be cool and into the same things as they are. Students want responsible adults who care about them, model successful adult development, and provide the necessary structure for them to grow and learn.

On a deeper level, teachers who *depend* on the love and friendship of their students are treading on a socio-emotional minefield. I hope I am not putting too fine a point on this argument. I am trying to convince you that you will indeed require intrinsically satisfying experiences in order to be motivated to do the hard work of teaching. It is important to acknowledge that relationships with students, co-workers, and parents can be a vital source of intrinsic motivation. I think healthy relationships are the linchpin that holds the teaching and learning process together—hence the emphasis on teaching as a human activity that this book is all about. But, I am trying to alert you to the vulnerability you expose yourself to if you depend on receiving unconditional love from your students. If you need to have your students' love you in order to feel job satisfaction, your chances of success are slim. As Metz (1993) warns, to rely on this kind of intrinsic reward in teaching, "is to build one's house on shifting sands" (p. 105).

To conclude on a high note, I will give some examples of possible scenarios in which super meaningful connections are experienced between teachers and students. These are meant to emphasize the point that teaching has the potential to be an exhilarating human endeavor for those who commit do doing it for the right reasons. This is also meant to provide a counterpoint to demonstrate the folly of expecting to be loved by students and making the reception of that love the primary intrinsic motivation for teachers' work.

- Mrs. Anderson asks Johnny to stay in from recess. It is the first 6-weeks of school, and Mrs. Anderson works one-on-one with each of her first grade students during recess periods. They sit together, and the teacher shows Johnny a book called *Splash!* She reads the book to him, pointing to the words as she reads. Then she asks Johnny to read it with her. Johnny focuses on the marks on the page that stand for "splash" and figures out that letters put into certain sequences consistently stand for the same words. By the third time through *Splash!*, he was able to read virtually all the words in this repeatable text. By the time recess was over, Johnny knew in his head and his heart that he was a reader. He was thrilled that he had solved the mystery of words on a page and has never forgotten these magic moments with Mrs. Anderson, counting this 20-minute learning experience as among the most important of his life.

• Miss Naccarato organized all the instruction in her middle-school social studies classes around themes. One of the most elaborate units was built around producing a puppet show from scratch based on a study of ancient civilizations. Students had to explore the relevant history, write the script, build the puppet stage, make the puppets, assign roles, memorize parts, and put on the performance. John was all but invisible in school. He kept to himself and was more interested in his personal reading and playing basketball at lunch than keeping up with schoolwork. As the class organized for the theme study of ancient civilizations, Miss Naccarato subtly alerted the other students to John's strengths as an avid reader and able writer, setting him up to have a significant role behind the scenes of the production. His puppet (the Saracen Messenger) was pretty lame, and he only had one line to speak in the actual show; still, he was grateful to Miss Naccarato for knowing him well enough to set up learning situations in which he was able to engage with others by exercising his strengths.

• Mr. Young asked Amos to come by his classroom after school. Since Mr. Young's Civics class was the only course he was sure to pass during the final term of his senior year, Amos wondered why he was being summoned. Turns out, the first thing Mr. Young asked was, "Do you think you are smart?" His teacher was not phrasing "smart" as in "smart ass" or "smart aleck;" he was asking a straight-up question. Amos did not know how to answer. Mr. Young told Amos that he had heard that his scores on the college entrance exam were among the highest in the school and he had looked up his grades. He found that the Amos's transcript included grades from A to F. He was on pace to graduate (if he stopped cutting classes), but Mr. Young expressed astonishment and dismay that Amos was working so far below his apparent potential. He asked if Amos was planning to go to college, to which the young man replied that he had not thought about it as a real possibility and did not know how he could possibly do it because his parents could never afford the bill. As a result of this conversation, Mr. Young got

Amos hooked up with a school counselor who found a college that would take Amos, showed him how to apply for admissions, and helped him qualify for grants-in-aid and work study financial support. Amos never thought of himself as smart or believed he could go to college until that meeting with Mr. Young. Making that intervention happen was not part of Mr. Young's job description, but it changed the trajectory of Amos's life.

These vignettes describe events that changed my own educational life—indeed, my existential life! Just as I was called by different names at different stages across my school career, so did I have different needs and receive different gifts from caring, savvy, dedicated teachers. I love the memory of these special moments. As they were happening, my teachers and I were tacitly aware that something important was going on—something that was felt, not spoken. Not one of these exceptional educators was hoping or expecting to win my affection by their actions. They were doing the job of teaching the only way they knew how. I love what these special people did for me, and I love knowing that opportunities to create moments like these are within the reach of every teacher. Taking advantage of these opportunities will generate the best intrinsic motivation for teaching I can imagine. You can love teaching without being dependent on the love of your students.

REFERENCES

Hatch, J. A. (1999). What preservice teachers can learn from studies of teachers' work. *Teaching and Teacher Education, 15*, 229–242.

Linsin, M. (2011, July 5). *Why you should never, ever be friends with students.* Smart Classroom Management. https://www.smartclassroommanagement.com/2011/05/07/never-be-friends-with-students/

Lloyd, C. (2016, July 1). *What is your parenting style?* GreatSchools.org. https://www.greatschools.org/gk/articles/types-of-parenting-styles/

Metz, M. H. (1993). Teachers' ultimate dependence on their students. In J. W. Little & M. W. McLaughlin (Eds.), *Teachers' work: Individuals, colleagues, and contexts* (pp. 106–136). Teachers College Press.

Organisation for Economic Co-operation and Development. (2015). *Education at a glance 2015.*

Planned Parenthood. (2010, August 16). *I'm 15, and I want to have a baby. Am I too young?* Planned Parenthood. https://www.plannedparenthood.org/learn/teens/ask-experts/

Strauss, V. (2018, November 15). Where in the world are teachers most respected? Not in the U.S., a new survey shows. *Washington Post.* https://www.washingtonpost.com/education/2018/11/15/where-world-are-teachers-most-respected-not-us-new-survey-shows/

Will, M. (2018, September 5). Teachers are paid almost 20 percent less than simi-
    lar professionals, analysis finds. *Education Week*. https://blogs.edweek.org/
    edweek/teacherbeat/2018/09/teachers_wage_penalty.html
Woods, P. (1987). Managing the primary teacher's role. In S. Delamont (Ed.), *The
    primary school teacher* (pp. 120–143). Falmer.

CHAPTER 19

LONE RANGER TEACHERS MAY SEEM HEROIC; BUT EVERYONE NEEDS SUPPORT, ENCOURAGEMENT, AND A SENSE OF COMMUNITY

I have mentioned my first teaching job in Kansas City in previous chapters. I loved the second graders I taught, I was proud to be a member of a dedicated faculty, and I was gratified to be accepted by the community surrounding the school. I was really happy to be teaching and delighted to be doing work that I thought was important. I always counted my time in Kansas City as some of the best years of my life, and I still do. But reflecting back, I have a different perspective now than I had at the time. I have come to understand that I was thinking, talking, and acting like what might be called a "lone White hero" (Emdin, 2016).

During my first year in Kansas City, I was literally the lone White teacher in the building. The system was one of the last major school districts in the United States to desegregate, and that process was due to begin in the year following my initial hire. When I interviewed for the job, I specifically requested an assignment in what were then called the "management" (read "all-Black") schools. My mindset was that the most important work to be done by teachers was in schools with the most need. For me, that meant urban schools for under-served populations.

Teaching as a Human Activity: Ways to Make Classrooms Joyful and Effective
pp. 173–180
Copyright © 2021 by Information Age Publishing
173

One year prior to moving to Missouri, while I was wrapping up my undergrad teacher preparation, I applied for a position with Teacher Corp, a domestic version of the Peace Corp. While the Peace Corp sent volunteers to serve people in developing nations, the Teacher Corp sent teachers to work in hard-to-staff schools. I was rejected because I already had the teaching credentials the program was designed to make possible; but I was committed to Teacher Corp aims, including the requirement that teachers live in the communities in which they work.

After finishing my degree at the University of Utah, I moved to Lees Summit, Missouri, a bedroom community outside of Kansas City. But, after just three months of teaching in the urban center of Kansas City, my world turned upside down. I cut all my ties in the suburbs and moved into an apartment in the community in which I was teaching. I lived across the street from a dance club called the Inferno (it was the 70s) and two doors down from a rhythm and blues venue called the Town Hall Ballroom. The only other White people around were two female sex workers who lived in my building.

I immersed myself in the Black community. I spent time on the stoop with my Black neighbors, I went to Black parties, I dated Black women, I listened to Black music, I smoked Kool cigarettes. Kansas City teachers went on strike during the second year I was there, and I remember describing my circumstances to a young White woman as we marched the picket line outside the school board building. Her condescending reaction was, "Oh, you are just trying to be Black!" I dismissed her comment at the time, and I still do not think it captures what was going on. What I have come to believe is more troublesome. At some level, I think I was trying to distinguish myself as one of the few White folks committed enough to live and work in Black settings.

I recall visiting one of my mentoring professors at the University of Utah during the summer after my first year in Kansas City. I showed Ladd Holt pictures of my students, my girlfriend and her daughter, my school, and my apartment building, in effect documenting my heroic White teacher status. He was wise and kind, allowing me to glower in my self-satisfaction. Other friends and relatives were less excited about my new life, some openly worrying about my physical safety. One uncle (also a teacher) actually asked what it was like to teach "those little pickaninnies." All this reaction only convinced me further that I was a special person doing special work.

When I left Kansas City for Jacksonville, I again asked for a position in the city center and moved into a neighborhood near the school to which I was assigned. Who knows the deep-seated psychosocial motives that drove me to want to teach exclusively in hard-to-staff schools in urban settings? I grew up in poverty, so I have considered that I was carrying around a kind of survivor's guilt, wanting to "give back" to justify my escape in place of others did not make it out. I have also worried that I have never been comfortable being around individuals who come from more affluent backgrounds, so I gravitated to schools for less privileged students; or perhaps I *was* just trying to be Black. In any case, the point I want to make from this long narrative is that setting yourself us a "lone ranger," out to save less fortunate others, may seem like an heroic quest, but doing so can be precarious for you, insulting to the communities you claim to serve, and detrimental to your students.

I was young, idealistic, and selfish. I tied my identity to being the only one who "gets it," the only one who really cares about kids enough to not sell out, the only one willing to do what is right. I do not feel bad about the young or idealistic part—I was always a slow developer, and I am still idealistic. I have no regrets about the work I did or the relationships I formed—I am only sorry that I was so into me and what the whole experience meant for me that I did not think about what my stance as a lone White hero might mean for my students, colleagues, and friends.

Years later, I recall watching the movie *Freedom Writers* and squirming throughout because I saw so much of myself in the Michelle Pfeiffer role of a White savior of poor, Black high-school kids. This and other films that valorize White teachers saving children of color (e.g., *Dangerous Minds* or *Up the Down Staircase*) are based on the same assumptions that I was living out in Kansas City and early on in Jacksonville. Hughey (2015) describes the typical elements of the broader genre of "White Savior" films as,

> A White person (the savior) enters the milieu and through their sacrifices, as a teacher, mentor, lawyer, military hero, aspiring writer, or wannabe Native American warrior, is able to physically save—or at least morally redeem—the person or community of folks of color. (p. 1)

What gets left out of such films is the fact that people of color and their children do not need saving, and that it is ethnocentric and self-serving to believe that it should be White people doing the saving (Vera & Gordon, 2003).

I want to broaden the frame so I can talk directly to more readers than White teachers who feel called to teach in schools serving Black kids. Teachers from any racial or cultural background can take on the persona of a "lone ranger teacher" who has special capabilities and attitudes that make it possible for him or her to accomplish things ordinary teachers cannot do. Setting aside that this is probably a self-serving illusion, teachers are much more effective when they have a stable network of support on which they can rely. Teaching, especially teaching that goes beyond routine expectations, is difficult work. Lone ranger teachers are likely to burn out while tilting at windmills.

I am old enough to remember watching the original *Lone Ranger* series on a tiny black and white television. Each week, the tall, White, and handsome lead actor would ride into a new frontier town, with Tonto ("his faithful Indian companion") close behind. The star wore a super-sharp western costume of all-white (save his trademark black mask), had a brilliant white horse named Silver, and brandished ivory handled pistols that fired silver bullets (but only when necessary). The show ended the same way every week: The town's problem was solved by our hero. One of the townspeople asked, "Who was that masked man?" Someone answered, "Why he's the Lone Ranger!" And the star brought his white steed to its hind legs and shouted, "Hi ho Silver, away!"

The symbolism embedded in this popular series has become part of American folklore. I could go off on the place of Tonto as the indigenous sidekick, or focus on how the search for a "silver bullet" has become part of the lexicon for solving complicated problems with simple solutions, or push more deeply into all the white and silver markers employed by the producers. But not here. What I want to spend a little time doing to is to think about what comparisons might apply when we think about what it might mean to be a "lone ranger teacher."

First, as I described in my narrative about teaching in Kansas City and Jacksonville, lone ranger teachers separate themselves from others. Like the masked man in the oater serial, they see themselves as uniquely suited for doing difficult work that others are incapable of getting done. They have special knowledge, skills, and commitments that make them capable of solving problems that others cannot solve. Those incapable others include members of communities the lone ranger teachers ride into and the professionals already working there.

Lots of times, lone ranger teachers seek out work settings that include populations that are perceived to be difficult to reach (e.g., English language learners, special education students, children of poverty, students from minority backgrounds, Native Americans, etc.). Sometimes, they internalize their heroic status and imagine that their special contributions are the only positives in the lives of those they are rescuing. Occasionally, lone ranger teachers spend 2 or 3 years in these settings, then ride on to greener pastures in education or other endeavors. Take a look at the literature that tracks "Teach for America" (aka, "Teach for Awhile") graduates for a salient example of the latter phenomenon (e.g., Naison, 2013; Ravitch, 2010).

Some of you may be asking: What is so wrong about being a lone ranger teacher? You have been preaching about how important teachers are and how proud we should be of the important work we do to support the development of young human beings. You seemed happy to tell your story of being the lone White teacher in Kansas City. So what are we to make of this metaphoric connection to a TV show from the 1950s?

For me, there is a kind of paradox at work here. Being able to produce high quality teaching in any setting is going to require a caring commitment to your work, your students, and their communities. We need teachers who want to be where they are and who expect to make a significant difference in the lives of those with whom they interact. But there is an important distinction between "making a difference" in people's lives and "saving" them. When this line gets blurred, teachers seek to work in settings in which they see their students, parents, and communities as inherently deficient—in need of fixing, in need of redeeming, in need of saving. These teachers adopt an attitude similar to that of colonizers taking lands from indigenous peoples, an attitude that sets them up as cultural superiors who are bringing civilization to barbarians (Viruru, 2005).

We sometimes saw this kind of "savior" motivation in applicants for our urban-multicultural teacher education program. When asked what they thought were the greatest obstacles facing teachers today, some prospective teachers would reveal in writing or in their face-to-face interviews that the biggest problem was that parents do not know how or do not care enough to properly raise their kids or that children in certain communities lacked the guidance and role models they needed to overcome their backgrounds. These applicants were sure that they could save their future students from the pervasively negative environments provided by their students' families and communities. Some of these eager future teachers openly talked about teaching as a religious calling, apparently assuming that there were folks out there in need of salvation.

We did not automatically reject applicants who expressed these kinds of attitudes, but we always questioned them closely about their motives and sometimes recommended other programs as a better fit. It is not a surprise that a good number of our mostly White, mostly well-educated, mostly middle-class applicants saw the mostly Black and Brown, mostly underserved, mostly poor clients of our program as "less than normal." That is how they are portrayed by certain political groups, depicted in the media, and maintained in the public consciousness. In fact, many charitable, religious, and educational organizations operate on the assumption that they have the means to save those they want to serve from the inadequacies and evils that surround them.

So, it is understandable that many bright, committed folks who want to teach have internalized a deficit perspective (Gorski, 2011) regarding those who are different from themselves. Even the preservice teachers who came to us with all the right reasons for wanting to teach in urban schools still talked about the amazement (sometimes dismay) of friends and family that they had chosen to work with kids who were destined to be difficult because of their deficient backgrounds. But, just because these beliefs are pervasive does not make it right to look past or accept them.

The point here is to warn you that thinking of yourself as a lone ranger teacher can include an unexamined desire to rescue children and young people from their own cultural experiences. That source of motivation is misplaced and situates you in an untenable position in relation to your students and their families at the same time it sets you up for failure as a teacher. Kids in every setting need the sense that they are capable people who can learn and grow with your support. Families in every setting need to feel respected and know that their participation is valued, whatever form that participation may take. Communities in every setting need to see you as an ally, doing your level best to build on all the strengths that support children's learning and development.

No matter where you teach, it is never your job to judge the parents or communities of your students. No one wants your pity. No one wants a condescending attitude. No one wants you to act like you know more about what is best for their children than they do. I vividly remember buying a coat for one of my second graders in Kansas City, taking it to her apartment on a cold evening during Christmas break, and having her mother take it from my hand and close the door without a word. She did not have to speak. I could see in her eyes that she thought I was presumptuous as hell, as in: "Who do you think you are? Why would you ever think it is your place to decide what my child needs? How dare you assume that I cannot take care of my own family?" At the time, I rationalized that I had done a good thing because my student got something I thought she needed; but hindsight, maturity, and experience have taught me to be a little wiser and a lot more humble. I figured out there are ways to help families access resources they might need without putting myself in the role of a personal benefactor who expects to glow in the warmth of his own benevolence.

Adopting a lone ranger positionality makes the possibility of making the powerful human connections necessary for the kind of teaching you want to do difficult at best. All the advice and practical ideas in this book will mean little unless you can join with your students and their families in a joint effort to maximize every learning opportunity available. Riding into town on a white horse with a gun belt full of silver bullets to solve the townspeople's problems will not cut it. Great teaching is based in great relationships—great human connections that exhilarate and benefit everyone involved. Relationships will be sterile and inert if you see yourself as a kind of lone ranger; but I want to say a little more about the "lone" part.

There is something quixotic about having a mission that no one else quite understands or is willing to make sacrifices to achieve. The term "quixotic" comes from the Spanish novel, *Don Quixote*, whose main character is full of romantic notions and unrealistic schemes. Like the Lone Ranger, Don Quixote had a faithful companion (Sancho Panza) who played a secondary role similar to Tonto; but otherwise, the two protagonists worked alone. There is no denying the attraction of being the "only one." We all want to stand for something, and we all want acknowledgment that we are unique; but setting yourself up as the only one who is doing what is right for kids or is willing to work in certain settings is a little pretentious and a lot risky.

We went over the pretentious part above. The risky part is that when you are alone, you cut yourself off from feedback and support that you need. I confessed early on in this book that I am an introvert—I am just fine with spending time by myself and am uncomfortable with folks I do not know well. But, that does not mean that I do not need and value the close human connections around me. My friends, colleagues, and especially my family are essential elements of all dimensions of my life. As a classroom teacher, professor, and scholar, I have always tried to break my own trail—and that sometimes led me to cut myself off from others. But, I have learned that being alone can mean living in a echo chamber of your own thoughts and feelings. It can mean being lonely.

No matter their social disposition, everyone needs human contact in order to receive feedback about what they are thinking, doing, and feeling. Indeed, our contact with others is a big part of what makes us human. We act, others react, and we shape future behavior based on those reactions (see Chapter 12). We express our humanity in our interactions with others. Teachers who work with children and young people need connections to other adults in order to maintain some perspective on their personal and professional lives. Whether extroverts, introverts, or something in between, everyone needs some kind of social contact with others in order not to feel isolated. Teachers who work alone can become lonely, depressed, and burned out.

Maintaining strong social networks is important for everyone and essential for teachers. My experience as an educator and mentor of educators is that these social networks can take many forms. Of course, face-to-face connections with colleagues who share your values and commitments can be especially meaningful when things go wrong or you need to celebrate. My former students virtually always used social media platforms to communicate during and after their teacher preparation. They continue to stay in touch and find it satisfying and comforting to be able to share their successes and vent their frustrations with old friends and trusted colleagues. Many of my most influential colleagues and valued friends are people I rarely see face to face—folks I have met at conferences or have communicated electronically with regarding our shared professional interests. I think teachers should join professional organizations and participate in conferences and on-line events so they can find support and develop camaraderie with like-minded educators who may be far away.

It is wonderful that you have joined in an effort to make the world a better place, but it is presumptuous and insulting to think of yourself as bringing redemption to those in need of fixing. It is perfectly fine to know that the work you want to do is as important as any on earth, but it is a mistake not to connect with and learn from others who bring their own insights, talents, and commitments to that work. Bottom line, it might seem romantic to be think of yourself as the "only one," but it is wiser to surround yourself with as much support and love as you can to keep your teaching dreams alive.

REFERENCES

Emdin, C. (2016). *For White folks who teach in the hood … and the rest of y'all too: Reality pedagogy and urban education.* Beacon Press.

Gorski, P. C. (2011). Unlearning deficit ideology and the scornful gaze: Thoughts on authenticating the class discourse in education. *Counterpoints, 402,* 152–173.

Hughey, M. W. (2015, January 19). The Whiteness of Oscar night. *Contexts.* https://contexts.org/blog/the-whiteness-of-oscar-night/

Naison, M. (2013, February 11). *Why Teach for America isn't welcome in my class.* AlterNet. http://www.alternet.org/education/why-teach-for-america-isnt-welcome-in-my-class

Ravitch, D. (2010). *The death and life of the great American school system: How testing and choice are undermining education.* Perseus.

Vera, H., & Gordon, A. M. (2003). *Screen saviors: Hollywood fictions of Whiteness.* Rowman & Littlefield.

Viruru, R. (2005). The impact of postcolonial theory on early childhood education. *Journal of Education, 35,* 1–28.

CHAPTER 20

GREAT TEACHERS MUST NOT BURN OUT; WE NEED THEM TO GUARD THE MEANING

There is a direct relationship between how much teachers want to make a difference and the rate of burnout. Highly committed, hard working teachers who come to teaching because they want their work lives to have significance are especially vulnerable for being disappointed when they start teaching in settings that make it difficult to develop the sense that they are fulfilling their dreams. Some argue that teachers need a better idea of the difficulties of contemporary teaching before they start—then they are supposed to lower their expectations and not burn out because they knew what they were getting into. This chapter takes the position that knowledge of the difficulties of teaching is necessary, but that the passion, energy, and pure joy that come with a deep commitment to making a difference in the world should be nurtured, celebrated, and supported. This chapter summarizes and reinforces the theme of the book that at its best, teaching is an inherently human activity and that great teachers are needed to guard the meaning that is sorely needed in today's schooling.

Studies of teacher attrition consistently show that more than 50% of new teachers leave the profession within their first five years in the classroom (Will, 2018). To me, this is stunning, scary, and sad. It is stunning because of the mere magnitude. What is going on that makes so many people turn away from what most who enter the field see as a calling? It is

Teaching as a Human Activity: Ways to Make Classrooms Joyful and Effective
pp. 181–189
Copyright © 2021 by Information Age Publishing
All rights of reproduction in any form reserved.

scary because schools are constantly breaking in a new set of novice professionals. It takes time, energy, and resources to initiate new teachers into the field (Garcia & Weiss, 2019). It is sad because of the emotional cost for those who leave. Teachers who leave the classroom early are often among the most committed and most talented (McFeely, 2018). It hurts my heart to think that their dreams of making a difference in the lives of their students did not come true.

Of course, not every teacher who leaves early is talented or committed; and not every exceptional teacher leaves because she or he is burned out. Still, there is a relationship between having high hopes for making a difference and the risk of burning out. It has to do with the depth of disappointment experienced when expectations are very high in the face of low levels of fulfillment. If you do not expect much from an experience, then you are less likely to be let down. If your hopes are sky-high, you have a lot farther to fall.

Applying criteria developed by Montero-Marín and García-Campayo (2010), teachers who put a great deal of time and effort into their work and are extremely dedicated and personally engaged in their teaching are more susceptible to burning out. My position has never been that we should lower new teachers' expectations for what they can accomplish in their careers and thereby make them less vulnerable to burning out. Teachers' aspirations for doing important work in a critically important field provide the energy that makes our profession special. I have (and will below) argued that teachers need balance in their lives so that they do not work themselves so hard that they jeopardize their physical and mental health; but I have never downplayed the hard work and extra time it takes to be a successful teacher.

I do not think we should either try to scare potential teachers away from the profession by emphasizing the reasons why teaching is difficult work or try to sugarcoat our job by failing to alert teachers-to-be about the potential stressors associated with classroom teaching. In the late 1990s, I had the chance to serve as a visiting professor at the Queensland University of Technology in Brisbane, Australia. While there, I collaborated with two amazing colleagues and friends, Sue Grieshaber and Gail Halliwell, on a study of teaching as an occupation. A big part of my time was spent completing a review of the international literature on teachers' work. I decided to report findings from that review in the form of an article for teachers of future teachers, entitled, "What preservice teachers can learn from studies of teachers' work" (Hatch, 1999). Going back to that piece helped me see that it is still important to give new and prospective teachers a heads-up about what to expect down the road. In the next paragraphs, I identify some of the salient characteristics of teachers' work from the original article and bring them up to date, citing more recent literature. It will be clear that these characteristics overlap, but taking them one at a time foreground the difficulties teachers face.

Uncertainty. Teaching is uncertain because it requires teachers to make myriad decisions on the fly every day, without building in time to reflect on or assess the outcomes of those decisions. In the short term, it is hard to know what is effective because there are so many students whose needs require accommodation, so many issues that arise on the spot, so many expectations built into the job, and so many audiences to whom the teacher must pay attention. In the long term, students move on and teachers rarely get to see if their hard work has paid off. In other occupations, the products of one's efforts are self evident. This is not always the case for teaching, leading some teachers to feel uncertain about their effectiveness. Overall, it is hard for teachers to be certain that they are pinpointing what students need, selecting appropriate content, and developing effective learning activities. Teachers cannot be sure how their lessons will play out in the classroom or what students will learn from them, and this uncertainty can cause anxiety (Campbell, 2007).

Complexity. Marilyn Cochran-Smith (2003) writes that, "*Teaching is unforgivingly complex.* It is not simply good or bad, right or wrong, working or failing" (p. 4, emphasis in original). Classrooms are busy places, and just keeping track of what is going on with a large number of people is difficult. The complexity of teaching is multiplied because teachers are responsible for much more than just academic development. Every action a teacher makes is filtered through the realization that children's social, psychological, physical, moral, as well as cognitive development are in play. Teachers have to balance the needs of individual students with those of the group; they have to make sense of sometimes contradictory roles (e.g., encourager versus evaluator); and they have to find ways to challenge students without defeating them. Further, there is ample evidence that teachers' work has intensified over the years as academic requirements are increased, accountability is ratcheted up, and new programs are implemented (Stone-Johnson, 2016). The impact of all this complexity is magnified because teachers do their work in real time, without the luxury of retreating to an office to look stuff up or consult with other specialists.

Isolation. The egg-crate architecture of most schools and the ways schedules are arranged make it unlikely that teachers will have the opportunity to interact with other professionals during the day. Further, it is part of school lore that teachers (from their first day on the job) are supposed to close their doors and take full responsibility for their classrooms. So, much of teachers' work is done in isolation. This was true when my original article was published, and it remains true today (Heasley & Smith, 2019). A nationwide study found that teachers spend only about three percent of their teaching day collaborating with colleagues, meaning that, "the majority of American teachers plan, teach, and examine their practice alone" (Mirel & Goldin, 2012, p. 1). The isolated nature of teachers' work can lead to feelings of abandonment and uncertainty, and the expectation that they should be able to work things out on their own makes it more difficult for teachers who may be struggling to reach out for support and assistance.

Lack of Autonomy. In other professions, practitioners are trusted to make decisions about what they will do and how they will do it. The expectation is that they are licensed because they have expert knowledge and they are expected to apply it professionally. Not so much for teachers. Teachers' lack of autonomy was real at the turn of the century, and studies show that it has actually decreased over the past two decades (Lamb-Sinclair, 2017; Walker, 2016). Not having the ability to decide what to teach, how to teach it, and how to assess their own effectiveness is one of the main sources of job dissatisfaction among teachers and a major reason they get burned out and quit. Interviewed by Tim Walker (2016), Richard Ingersoll of the University of Pennsylvania summarizes:

> The data consistently show us that a big issue is how much voice, how much say, do teachers have in the decisions that affect their jobs? Teachers are micromanaged. They have been saying for a long time that one size *does not* fit all, all students are different. But they are told to stick to the scripted curriculum, which might work for a weaker teacher but it drives good teachers nuts. (p. 2)

Stress. The original article synthesized the research of the day, identifying conditions that made teaching stressful work. A partial list included the following elements:

> poor physical condition of schools, lack of autonomy, unreasonable workloads, insufficient time to meet expectations, increases in children's needs, additional nonteaching responsibilities, increased difficulties with parents, poor inservice training, inadequate school management, increased accountability, and added responsibility for children with disabilities. (Hatch, 1999, p. 233)

These negative factors remain in place, and many have gotten worse. It is no wonder that teaching routinely ranks among the most stressful of occupations (Busby, 2019). Recent studies tell us that upward of 90% of teachers are experiencing stress on the job, and many are experiencing stress levels that make it hard to cope in the classroom (Herman et al., 2018).

In the next section of this chapter, I will talk about ways teachers, especially new teachers, can be successful (and even thrive) in the face of characteristics that make teaching such challenging and stressful work. Part of my aim is forewarn new teachers about some of potential pitfalls so they can be forearmed and go in with their eyes open. When I asked novice and experienced teachers what they thought about exposing new and future teachers to my research on teachers' work, almost all said it was a good idea. Here are snippets of their responses, reported as part of my 1999 article:

- "I think it should be taught so students will not go into the profession blindly."
- "It made me realize that my fears as a teacher are shared by others."
- "By being aware of these issues, future teachers will be better prepared to handle their feelings and worries." (Hatch, 1999, pp. 238–239)

The big point here matches a major impetus for this book: We need great teachers to flourish and stay in the profession, rather than burn out and take their talents elsewhere. The best teachers have the biggest dreams. I do not want those dreams to be set aside when the going gets tough.

Overcoming Uncertainty. Yes, there are lots of unknowns associated with teaching; but what can be known is right in front of you every day. You do not have to rely on your students' scores on end-of-year standardized tests to know if they are learning. Assessment should be an organic part of the teaching and learning process—you teach kids to do stuff they cannot do, you have them show you they can do it, then you both celebrate. You do not have to receive a shout out from a famous person to know that you are having a profound impact on your students' lives. You can feel the importance of the human contacts that you have every day with the young people you teach. When your class is able to work in concert to achieve shared goals, there is an electricity that lights up the moment. Children may not remember the exact moments that changed their lives, but those moments happened and those changes are real. You can be certain that what you are doing is vital to your students and the future of our society. You can be certain in your heart of hearts that you are doing all you can to make decisions that benefit the children and young people you are lucky enough to teach. You can be certain that expressing the breadth of your humanness in the classroom will open the doors to success for you and your students.

Unraveling Complexity. Yes, teaching is a complex activity; but focusing on essential elements that make classrooms places where human learning is accomplished and celebrated can keep teachers from being overwhelmed. Stripped to its bare bones, the methodological part of teaching is comprised of what your students need to learn, how you can best make that learning happen, and how you will know if your teaching has been successful—what traditional textbooks call curriculum, instruction, and assessment. Knowing all you can about each of these areas as well as taking into account what your system expects from you in each dimension is important. That means making sense of complex and sometimes contradictory information. As has been highlighted in several places in this book, I think you can cut through the clutter by focusing on (1) implementing curriculum based on where *your students* are operating and what comes next; (2) providing the scaffolded experiences they need in order to advance their knowledge and skills; and (3) building in activities that give students the opportunity to experience, demonstrate and celebrate their newfound mastery. Demystifying the social, psychological, and moral complexities that abound in classrooms means knowing and communicating who you are, why you are there, and what you expect to accomplish. Again, following the advice in previous chapters would mean setting up classroom communities in which everyone has a shared understanding of why they are there, everyone is invested in everyone else's success, and everyone knows that nothing less than everyone's personal best will be acceptable.

Resisting Isolation. Yes, there are physical, institutional and traditional barriers that isolate teachers one from another; but creating and maintaining relationships with others who are committed to supporting you can help breach these barriers. One way to think about the human connections that everyone needs is to imagine expanding circles that start with those who are most near to you and working out to those who may be far away. Those nearest are usually loved ones and family—as in spouses, partners, parents, siblings. They are likely not teachers themselves, but their understanding and unconditional support can be vital to keeping you from feeling alone. Close friends and confidants represent the next circle out. These individuals might be teachers, but not necessarily; but for sure, they need to be people with whom you can be absolutely honest about your feelings and frustrations—trusting them to be honest in return without being judgmental. You also need positive working relationships with colleagues. This can include other professionals at your school (i.e., teachers, administrators, counselors, supervisors, secretaries). These may not always be close friends, but they have insider knowledge of the contexts in which you work and can provide insights and marshal resources that others might not be able to access. Moving out, the next circle could include professionals with whom you may not have regular face-to-face contact. This might mean participating in professional organizations, joining groups that discuss issues and share support on social media, or creating/following online blogs about the teaching experience. If you are feeling isolated, you need to reach out at as many of these levels as you can. Even better to establish and work at nurturing these supportive relationships in order to reduce your chances of feeling isolated from the get go.

Asserting Autonomy. Yes, teachers have far too little say in how they do their jobs; but competent, confident, responsible teachers can take charge of their work lives and increase their opportunities to make autonomous decisions in their classrooms. Being autonomous does not mean throwing out the "teacher proof" curriculum that teachers are often expected to implement, nor does it mean ignoring the standards that are going to be tested at the end of the year. It means taking what is given, understanding what is expected, knowing what is permissible, and making decisions about what you will do in the best interest of your students. In some schools, that might mean following the prescribed curriculum, but supplementing it with meaningful activities. It might mean covering the required standards, but in your own unique way. It might mean developing and implementing a curriculum based directly on the immediate needs of your students. At whatever level you are expressing your autonomy, you will need to be able to rationalize your decisions to your self, your students, their parents, and your supervisors. You can do that! You are a trained professional with knowledge, skills, and commitments that give you the competence to make tough decisions. You are confident in the knowledge that you are the one who knows best what your students need. You are a committed educator who is willing to take responsibility for maximizing the learning opportunities of all your students.

Coping With Stress. Yes, teaching is stressful; but there are ways to reduce the stress and manage your reactions to it. For me, it helps to realize that stress is not an inherently bad phenomenon. We all experience stress, and it can provide beneficial energy and motivation. However, when stress becomes intense or lasts for long periods of time, it can be debilitating and harmful to your physical and emotional health. My general advice is what I always say to myself when I am feeling stressed out: "Do something, even if it is wrong." This is a call to action, not a plea for stupidity. I did not say, "Do anything and hope it is not wrong." I want to consider my decisions carefully, including an analysis of possible consequences good and bad; but I do not expect every decision to be perfect so I go ahead and act rather than stew in my own anxiety. I think of stress as having two faces: the stressors and my reactions to them. Taking action to reduce some of the stressors surrounding teaching might mean asking your principal for additional support in dealing with issues related to parents, making a plan that rethinks how you organize your grading and preparation time, inviting the guidance counselor to observe and offer insights on your behavior management system, or consulting with special education teachers about providing for the needs of struggling students. You see the point. When you are feeling anxious, take a look at what is causing the stress and take action to reduce it. The other side of the stress formula is how you deal with it. We all have developed mechanisms for coping with stress—some healthy and some not. Experts agree that suggestions like the following are healthy ways to prevent or reduce chronic stress:

- rebalance work and home;
- build in regular exercise;
- eat well and limit alcohol and stimulants;
- connect with supportive people;
- carve out hobby time;
- practice meditation, stress reduction or yoga
- sleep enough;
- bond with your pet;
- take a vacation; and
- see a counselor, coach or therapist (Stoll, 2020, pp. 2–3).

Being aware of and finding ways to cope with the challenges of teaching is vital to your chances of success in the classroom. The profession and America's young people are depending on you to bring your energy, intelligence and commitment to school every day. We are depending on you to guard the meaning that is sometimes hard to find in contemporary schooling. We are depending on you to not become overwhelmed and burn out. In a very real sense, we would be lost if we lost you.

We need you to revive teaching as a meaningful human activity. Meaningful activities happen when humans share experiences that they know are important. Those shared experiences build and cement relationships that make future learning experiences even more joyful and effective. This is the kind of positive recursive cycle we need you to build so that you and your students come to see schooling as an exciting, fulfilling, and gratifying adventure. I am so grateful that you are in the most important profession in the world, and I hope the ideas in this book will inspire you and give you some useful tools for expressing the best of your humanness throughout your career.

REFERENCES

Busby, E. (2019). *Teachers suffer more stress than other workers, study finds.* The American Institute of Stress. https://www.stress.org/teachers-suffer-more-stress-than-other-workers-study-finds

Campbell, E. (2007). Glimpses of uncertainty in teaching. *Curriculum Inquiry, 37*(1), 1–8.

Garcia, E., & Weiss, E. (2019, April 16). *U.S. schools struggle to hire and retain teachers*. Economic Policy Institute. https://www.epi.org/publication/u-s-schools-struggle-to-hire-and-retain-teachers-the-second-report-in-the-perfect-storm-in-the-teacher-labor-market-series/

Hatch, J. A. (1999). What preservice teachers can learn from studies of teachers' work. *Teaching and Teacher Education, 15*(4), 229–242.

Heasley, J. R., & Smith, M. W. (2019, March 1). *Moving from isolation to collaboration in the classroom*. National Association of Secondary School Principals. https://www.nassp.org/2019/03/01/moving-from-isolation-to-collaboration-in-the-classroom/

Herman, K. C., Hickmon-Rosa, J., & Reinke, W. M. (2018). Empirically derived profiles of teacher stress, burnout, self-efficacy, and coping with associated student outcomes. *Journal of Positive Behavior Interventions, 20*(20), 90–100.

Lamb-Sinclair, A. (2017, September 10). Why teachers need their freedom. *The Atlantic*. https://www.theatlantic.com/education/archive/2017/09/why-teachers-need-their-freedom/539151/

McFeely, S. (2018, March 27). *Why your best teachers are leaving and 4 ways to keep them*. Gallup Education. https://www.gallup.com/education/237275/why-best-teachers-leaving-ways-keep.aspx

Mirel, J., & Goldin, S. (2012, April 12). Alone in the classroom: Why teachers are too isolated. *The Atlantic*. https://www.theatlantic.com/national/archive/2012/04/alone-in-the-classroom-why-teachers-are-too-isolated/255976/

Montero-Marín, J., & García-Campayo, J. (2010, June 6). A newer and broader definition of burnout. *BMC Public Health*. https://www.researchgate.net/publication/44651156_A_newer_and_broader_definition_of_burnout_Validation_of_the_Burnout_Clinical_Subtype_Questionnaire_BCSQ-36

Stoll, M. (2020). *10 simple ways to deal with stress*. Sutter Health. https://www.sutterhealth.org/health/mind-body/10-simple-ways-to-cope-with-stress

Stone-Johnson, C. (2016). Intensification and isolation: Alienated teaching and collaborative professional relationships in the accountability context. *Journal of Educational Change, 17*, 29–49.

Walker, T. (2016, January 11). *Teacher autonomy declined over past decade, new data shows*. NEA Today. https://www.nea.org/advocating-for-change/new-from-nea/teacher-autonomy-declined-over-past-decade-new-data-shows

Will, M. (2018, October 23). 5 things to know about today's teaching force. *Education Week*. https://blogs.edweek.org/edweek/teacherbeat/2018/10/today_teaching_force_richard_ingersoll.html

POSTSCRIPT

What Does Teaching as a Human Activity Look Like During a Time of Crisis?

It is January 21, 2021, the day after Joe Biden was inaugurated as the 46th president of the United States. I finished the body of this book 8 weeks ago, but it did not feel right to send it to the publisher without connecting it somehow to the health, economic, political, and educational crises that have defined the last 11 months. Eighty percent of this text was written since the COVID-19 pandemic began turning the world, including the lives of teachers, upside down. At this moment, thousands of Americans are dying from the coronavirus each day, hundreds of thousands are out of work, the country is reeling after domestic terrorists stormed the U.S. Capitol in a violent attempt to overturn the outcome of an election they did not like, and teachers are not sure where and how they will be teaching for the rest of the year. I did not want the book to be about teaching during a crisis, but it seems odd to just act like the earth-shaking events of the past year did not happen.

I am so thankful for all the teachers out there!

Thank you for …

- being there when kids need you most;
- staying flexible when the system is most rigid;
- keeping learning alive when it seems like an afterthought to others;
- doing your professional best when no one is looking;

Teaching as a Human Activity: Ways to Make Classrooms Joyful and Effective
pp. 191–199

- modeling mature adult behavior when it is hard to find elsewhere;
- holding schools together when other institutions are crumbling; and
- loving your job when it is harder than it has ever been.

Hang in there! This country and its children need you now!

This is a Facebook post I put up Thanksgiving morning, 2020. A great many of my Facebook friends are educators, most of them former students who are now teaching across the U.S. I hoped the post would make a small contribution to the morale of a group that sorely needed a boost, and I meant what I said in each line.

Whether teaching face to face, online, or in some hybrid combination, teachers have stepped up to the challenge that the Coronavirus pandemic threw down; and there is no doubt that students have sorely missed interactions with their teachers and the experiences that go with attending school. Teachers have had to stay flexible week to week as states and school systems decide what will be done, with whom, and how. Teachers have worked diligently to develop and deliver meaningful activities that engage their students and move them forward, while the obstacles for all students, especially special education, English as a second language, and poor students, keep piling up. Teachers have put in uncountable extra hours, going beyond the call of duty every day for months on end, often grinding through challenges in their own homes with only their immediate families to notice. Along with doctors and nurses, teachers have shown the world what responsible adults do during a crisis; and that kind of behavior was in short supply during 2020. Teachers have demonstrated how vital their roles are to holding schools and society together, while individuals in other institutions have abandoned their responsibilities, putting themselves first and everyone else at risk. Teachers have made it clear that their exemplary actions during the most difficult time in memory are based in a deep commitment to their profession, a profound love for their students, and undaunted devotion to the hard work of shaping America's future.

It is impossible to know exactly how the world will change as a result of the compounding effects of crises in health, economics, politics, and education. But it looks like it will change a lot. As a country and a collection of individuals, we have not done a good job of handing the Coronavirus pandemic. We know for sure that many Americans have been reluctant, even resistant, to follow the recommendations of scientists, doctors, and other health professionals when it comes to doing what is right for themselves, their families, and their fellow citizens. Thinking about the aims of this book, it seems clear that schools have to do a better job of helping students learn to sift through false and misleading information that abounds in the media, especially on the internet. As was emphasized in Chapter 15 and has become alarmingly clear over the past year, students need to develop critical thinking skills that will give them the power to make informed decisions about their own well-being and the health and safety of others based on fact-based information from legitimate sources.

There has been a kind of selfishness embedded in the health crisis as it played out that is very disturbing to me. Some of our leaders and too many ordinary Americans have thrown the most vulnerable of their fellow citizens under the bus, downplaying the severity of the pandemic and scoffing at precautions that would slow the transmission of the disease and reduce the death rate among vulnerable groups (Bernstein, 2020). Our self-centeredness as a nation has never been more apparent—as in "I am going to do what I want, where I want, with whomever I want—even it means you might get sick and die." If we are serious about thinking of teaching and learning as essential human activities, helping students learn the inherent value of the other humans seems critically important. Establishing "cooperation" as a central purpose of schooling so that working together is valued more than beating the other guy would help (Chapter 2); setting up classrooms as "communities of learning" where everyone has a stake in everyone else's success could help redirect selfishness (Chapter 3); and emphasizing "loving" as a human process would provide the opportunity to teach content, skills, and dispositions that enhance the best parts of our humanity (Chapter 8).

We do not know exactly what the long-term economic consequences of the crises of the past year will be; but we can make a good guess that things will be very different. The future of retail shopping and the viability of small businesses will almost certainly never be the same (D. Thompson, 2020). It looks like lots of jobs will just go away and many more will change dramatically. Software robots and other types of digital workers will have an increasing presence in the workplace and more and more employees will be working remotely (Bouquet, 2020). The job market of the future will favor those with more education, more technological savvy, and more flexibility.

As educators, we need to think carefully and act strategically to help ensure that our students are prepared to operate in an economy that is morphing even more rapidly than in the past because of the pandemic and our responses to it. As it relates to this book, the aims laid out in Chapters 14, 15, and 16 seem especially important. Kids need to learn how to think! Just mastering the basic skills and content that are tested on achievement tests will not cut it in the job market our students will enter. They will need to develop their brainpower and learn to value their ability to take in and process information from a variety of sources. They need to learn to apply their critical thinking capacities to assess the vast array of information available, and they need to understand the place of technology in their lives as workers, citizens, and human beings. The application of all the technologies surveyed in Chapter 16 is being accelerated because of current circumstances, so making sure that our students are prepared to shape inevitable technological advances so that they enhance and not diminishes our shared humanity is vital.

My heart was crushed as I watched the crazed mob rampage through the halls of the U.S. Congress on January 6, 2021. I knew that many Trump supporters who were lead to believe that the election had been rigged were frustrated and angry; but I had no idea that so many had been radicalized and were ready to take part in a violent insurrection. I never imagined that I would see the day when the institutions that have made our democracy unique among the world's governments would face direct assault from the ranks of its own leaders and its own citizens. As the images of the tyranny and the testimonies of those involved continue to come to light, my sense of loss and sorrow for my country only deepen. Wiser heads than me will have plenty to say about how and why our democracy has been pushed to the brink, but I am compelled to wonder what this all means for teachers and teaching?

Our democratic way of life continues to be under assault. The threat posed by white supremacists and other hate groups will not go away just because Donald Trump is no longer president. In the face of dozens of court decisions confirming that no evidence of voter irregularities exists, millions of ordinary people continue to believe conspiracy theories claiming that the 2020 election was fraudulent (McKelvey, 2021). Communities, congregations, friendships, and families are being torn apart because we cannot even engage in civil discourse. It turns out that in the current climate, certain divisive politicians, a wide swath of media outlets, and a remarkably large group of misguided citizens act as if they are not just entitled to their own opinions, they are entitled to their own facts. As mentioned above, schools have to do a better job of helping young people sift through the information available to them by providing the skills needed to make reasoned, sound judgments about the reliability of what they are being told (Chapters 15 and 16). Just as importantly, educators can act and teach in ways that challenge the ignorance and hatred that fuel the discontent exhibited by those who would undermine the rule of law and mock the democratic principles that have made our country a beacon of hope for the rest of the world. I am not talking about a whitewashed history curriculum or a revival of traditional civics classes, but a shift to schooling that emphasizes building on the humanity in each of us and celebrates the humanity of everyone around us. Applying the ideas in this book may not have an impact on the political craziness we see around us at this writing, but it offers some hope that things could be better for future generations.

This past year was the hardest period for teachers in my memory. Vaccines for COVID-19 are being distributed at this point and we have new leadership in Washington, but the rest of the 2020–2021 school year looks like it will continue to be disjointed at best. Teachers, students, and parents will have to continue adjusting to the ebbs and flows of the pandemic until it is finally brought under control. There has been no national leadership on how schools should handle the pandemic, and states and local authorities have been all over the map with their policies. In the spring of 2019, most school systems went to electronic learning (e-learning) with both teachers and students working from home when the first wave of cases started showing up. Some systems had e-learning modules already on hand, but most teachers were on their own, trying to figure out the technology, package the content, and engage their students. They went into this crazy time with no warning, little training, and minimal support. Some teachers worked with students who already had the hardware, tech savvy, and Wi-Fi capabilities needed for learning from home, but many others were responsible for teaching students who lacked the technological resources needed to successfully keep up.

With the start of a new academic year in fall 2020, most schools tried to reopen. Many offered parents the option of keeping their children at home for remote learning or sending them to school for face-to-face instruction. Some systems set up hybrid schedules, in which students attended school on some days and worked from home on others. The stress on teachers multiplied. Some were assigned to teach electronically from home, some did e-learning from school facilities, some met their classes in the schools (with varying degrees of protection from the virus), and many did some combination of electronic and face-to-face teaching. The press on teachers has never been greater. At the same time they have been super anxious about their own health and that of their families, teachers have been whiplashed by fluctuating policies and unreasonable expectations. Given the craziness of the times, teachers' efforts to do what is right for kids have been nothing short of heroic.

We have learned a lot about education from going through this health crisis. It is clear that students and young adults need to be in direct contact with their teachers in order to maximize their learning. All the indicators show an across the board learning loss from all the ups and downs of the pandemic; but the damage is most alarming among those who are already most at risk for being behind in school (i.e., students with disabilities, ESL students, and students from underserved communities) (Meckler & Natanson, 2020; C. Thompson, 2020). Clearly, kids are not learning as much in e-learning environments; but we are witnessing other negative outcomes when young people are not in school with their teachers and peers. Students report being bored, sad, lonely, frustrated, and angry because of the forced isolation caused by the pandemic (Natanson & Meckler, 2020), and health professionals worry that children and young adults' emotional well-being and social development may be jeopardized as a result of being separated from their peers and teachers (Goldberg, 2020).

The health crisis has shown the world that the role of teacher cannot be supplanted by technological innovation. Futurists have predicted that artificial intelligence, adaptive computer programs, and plugging into the internet will more effectively and efficiently teach the students of tomorrow, significantly reducing or eliminating the need for classroom teachers (Godsey, 2015; Stubbs, 2012). Those predictions have proven to be seriously flawed. Personalized learning is one example of an adaptive technology that has been widely utilized during the pandemic. Students sign into these programs and receive computer-based instruction tailored to where they are academically, as determined by continuous assessments that are built into the system. Prior to the pandemic, Paul Barnwell (2017), wrote about the impact of implementing a personalized learning program in his high school English classes:

> And as I have experienced firsthand, the role of teachers shifts dramatically with the adoption of these adaptive programs. Instead of a teacher striving to know a student on multiple levels—from understanding the nuances of his or her academic skills, to building positive relationships and crafting learning experiences based on more than numerical reading scores—educators are on the sidelines while a machine takes over. Personalized learning often becomes inherently impersonal; it is a sterile approach to messy, complex classroom processes. (p. 3)

The application of personalized learning and other computer-based technologies has expanded exponentially since the pandemic forced students to learn at home or in highly modified classroom environments. This provides a kind of natural experiment to determine the efficacy of replacing teachers with technological applications; and the results confirm that these "inherently impersonal" approaches are not meeting students' needs—not academically, socially, or emotionally. Human contact is vital to the teaching and learning process. As highlighted in Chapter 13, human beings learn best when their efforts are scaffolded by other human beings. A central element of effective teaching is joint engagement between someone who knows something important and someone who wants to learn it. No computer program, no matter how sophisticated and "intelligent," can take the place of the magic that happens when two human beings share the moment when something really important is accomplished. The cumulative loss of those moments because of the coronavirus pandemic will be felt for years to come.

Anticipating the abatement of these interconnected crises provides a genuine opportunity to rethink the ways we do school. As has been stressed throughout this book, we have an opportunity to make the experiences of students and teachers more human, thus elevating the meaningfulness and effectiveness of what we do. We have the opportunity to reconsider the purposes of school so that educators, students, parents and the public see compelling reasons for showing up, putting forth their best effort, and supporting schools in the United States (see Chapter 2). We have the opportunity to give teachers the professional recognition, respect, and autonomy they have earned, granting them their due in terms of decision making and earning power (Chapter 20). We have the opportunity to challenge the primacy of allowing testing regimes based on faulty assumptions and questionable applications (Hatch, 2015) to determine how much students are learning and how well teachers are teaching (Chapter 5). We have the opportunity to make technology work for us, rather than racing forward into a future that diminishes our opportunities to develop and express our humanity (Chapters 15 and 16).

At this writing, we have a new administration in Washington. We have new leadership in the White House and in the Department of Education. While it is impossible to know how much change will come about with these new players, it looks like things have a good chance of getting better. It looks like teachers will have more space to implement ideas like those found in this book. The primary aim of this book is to inspire teachers to make classrooms more joyful and effective by applying some basic suggestions that can help them and their students see the teaching and learning process as an essential expression of their humanness. Reflecting on these goals, I searched the internet for characteristics that define the best aspects of humanity. Looking across multiple lists, I synthesized a set of human traits that are most admired in human beings, ordering them from most cited on down. I then went into Merriam-Webster's online dictionary and found definitions for the positive human characteristics on the list. I also clicked on the antonyms button for each trait, and recorded those to help clarify what expressing these positive attributes looks like and does not.

Here is the list. I framed each contrasting set of elements as a question because it seems clear coming out of this difficult time that as individuals, as a society, and as educators, we have the responsibility to address these questions for the sake of our shared future. Will we strive to protect and nurture the best elements of our humanity or default to the worst?

- *Compassion* (sympathetic consciousness of others' distress together with a desire to alleviate it) or *Callousness* (indifference to suffering)?
- *Kindness* (exhibiting a sympathetic or helpful nature) or *Thoughtlessness* (careless disregard for the rights or feelings of others)?
- *Honesty* (fairness and straightforwardness of conduct) or *Deceitfulness* (the tendency or disposition to deceive or give false impressions)?
- *Trustworthiness* (worthy of confidence) or *Undependability* (unable to be trusted or relied on)?
- *Integrity* (firm adherence to a code of moral values) or *Evil* (exhibiting morally reprehensible actions)?
- *Humility* (freedom from pride or arrogance) or *Egoism* (excessive concern for oneself with exaggerated feelings of self-importance)?
- *Responsibility* (accepting moral, legal, or mental accountability) or *Recklessness* (taking action without proper caution and careless disregard for consequences)?

I want to stay positive about which way we are headed. I do see a genuine opportunity to make things better for students and teachers as we go into the rest of this decade; but I remain worried about general patterns in society and the destructive underside that has emerged from hiding over the past few years. Based on what I see all around me, I think the negative side of the contrasts I identified above has an increasingly troublesome hold on contemporary life (in our country and abroad). What keeps me awake at night is the fear that we are losing touch with the positive elements that bind us to our humanity.

Teachers cannot and should not be solely responsible for elevating compassion, kindness, honesty, trustworthiness, integrity, humility, and responsibility over their demoralizing counterparts; but we are in a position to try our best to make a meaningful difference. We have the opportunity to connect with our students in ways that demonstrate the power of human commitment to worthy goals. We have a forum for teaching the skills, knowledge and dispositions that future citizens will need in order to shape a more positive tomorrow. We have the chance to show students the critical importance of recognizing and celebrating the humanity in all of us. We have the responsibility to give our personal best each day, and to not let anything (not the bureaucracy, teacher proof curriculum, canned programs, standardized tests, accountability regimes, teacher evaluation schemes, technology for its own sake, a pandemic, or a political crisis) get between us and the most important job on the planet.

REFERENCES

Barnwell, P. (2017, February 15). Are teachers becoming obsolete? *The Atlantic*. https://www.theatlantic.com/education/archive/2017/02/becoming-obsolete/516732/

Bernstein, L. (2020, October 20). The coronavirus pandemic has caused nearly 300,000 more deaths than expected in a typical year. *Washington Post*. https://www.washingtonpost.com/health/coronavirus-excess-deaths/2020/10/20/1e1d77c6-12e1-11eb-ba42-ec6a580836ed_story.html

Bouquet, C. (2020, June). *How COVID-19 caused the future of work to arrive early*. Institute for Management Development. https://www.imd.org/research-knowledge/articles/How-COVID-19-caused-the-future-of-work-to-arrive-early/

Godsey, M. (2015, March 25). The deconstruction of the K–12 teacher: When kids can get their lessons from the Internet, what's left for classroom instructors to do? *The Atlantic*. https://www.theatlantic.com/education/archive/2015/03/the-deconstruction-of-the-k-12-teacher/388631/

Goldberg, E. (2020, November 12). Teens in Covid isolation: 'I felt like I was suffocating.' *New York Times*. https://www.nytimes.com/2020/11/12/health/covid-teenagers-mental-health.html

Hatch, J. A. (2015). *Reclaiming the teaching profession: Transforming the dialogue on public education*. Rowman & Littlefield.

Meckler, L., & Natanson, H. (2020, December 6). 'A lost generation': Surge of research reveals students sliding backward, most vulnerable worst affected. *Washington Post*. https://www.washingtonpost.com/education/students-falling-behind/2020/12/06/88d7157a-3665-11eb-8d38-6aea1adb3839_story.html?utm_campaign=wp_todays_headlines&utm_medium=email&utm_source=newsletter&wpisrc=nl_headlines

McKelvey, T. (2021, January 5). US election 2020: The people who still believe Trump won. *BBC*, https://www.bbc.com/news/world-us-canada-55481521

Natanson, H., & Meckler, L. (2020, November 26). Remote school is leaving children sad and angry: A rising emotional toll is hitting the youngest students hard. *Washington Post*. https://www.washingtonpost.com/education/2020/11/27/remote-learning-emotional-toll/?arc404=true

Stubbs, B. (2012, July 11). *Will technology make face to face learning redundant?* Education Technology Solutions. https://educationtechnologysolutions.com/2012/07/will-technology-make-face-to-face-learning-redundant/

Thompson, C. (2020, December 6). Schools confront 'off the rails' numbers of failing grades. *Associated Press*. https://www.yahoo.com/news/schools-confront-off-rails-numbers-161651110.html

Thompson, D. (2020, April 20). The pandemic will change American retail forever. *The Atlantic*. https://www.theatlantic.com/ideas/archive/2020/04/how-pandemic-will-change-face-retail/610738/

ABOUT THE AUTHOR

J. Amos Hatch is professor emeritus at the University of Tennessee. He began his career teaching in urban elementary schools in Kansas City, Missouri and Jacksonville, Florida. After earning his PhD, he shifted to teaching teachers and advanced graduate students at the Ohio State University campus in Marion, Ohio and the University of Tennessee in Knoxville. To date, Amos has published eight books, authored over 150 journal articles and book chapters, and presented scores of papers at academic conferences around the globe. His published work has been translated into Spanish, Chinese, and Korean. He was executive editor of two important education journals, served in leadership capacities in multiple professional organizations, and was the recipient of numerous awards for teaching, scholarship, and professional service. Although a prolific scholar, his first love is teaching and supporting others who love to teach.

Printed in Great Britain
by Amazon

23999298R00123